BASIC BANKRUPTCY LAW FOR PARALEGALS

FORMS MANUAL

Third Edition

David L. Buchbinder
Member, California and Pennsylvania Bars

Aspen Law & Business
A Division of Aspen Publishers, Inc.

ISBN 1-56706-512-0

This publication is designed to provide accurate and authoritative information in regard to the subject matter covered. It is sold with the understanding that the publisher is not engaged in rendering legal, accounting, or other professional services. If legal advice or other professional assistance is required, the services of a competent professional person should be sought.

> --From a <u>Declaration of Principles</u> jointly adopted by a Committee of the American Bar Association and Committee of Publishers and Associations.

1   2   3   4   5

NOTE: Each form is numbered to correspond to the chapter of the text in which the form is initially or primarily described. Where multiple forms accompany a chapter, the forms have been sequentially numbered.

The forms presented are representative examples only. Local rule or custom should be ascertained as to the specific requirements within a given district.

CONTENTS

FORM 4.1

Voluntary Petition

FORM 1. VOLUNTARY PETITION

United States Bankruptcy Court _____ District of _____	VOLUNTARY PETITION

IN RE (Name of debtor - If individual, enter Last, First, Middle)	NAME OF JOINT DEBTOR (Spouse) (Last, First, Middle)
ALL OTHER NAMES used by the debtor in the last 6 years (Include married, maiden, and trade names)	ALL OTHER NAMES used by the joint debtor in the last 6 years (Include married, maiden, and trade names)
SOC. SEC./TAX I.D. NO. (If more than one, state all)	SOC. SEC. TAX/I.D. NO. (If more than one, state all)
STREET ADDRESS OF DEBTOR (No. and street, city, state, and zip code)	STREET ADDRESS OF JOINT DEBTOR (No. and street, city, state, and zip code)
COUNTY OF RESIDENCE OR PRINCIPAL PLACE OF BUSINESS	COUNTY OF RESIDENCE OR PRINCIPAL PLACE OF BUSINESS
MAILING ADDRESS OF DEBTOR (If different from street address)	MAILING ADDRESS OF JOINT DEBTOR (If different from street address)

LOCATION OF PRINCIPAL ASSETS OF BUSINESS DEBTOR (If different from address listed above)	VENUE (Check one box) ☐ Debtor has been domiciled or has had a residence principal place of business, or principal assets in this District for 180 days immediately preceding the date of this petition or for a longer part of such 180 days than in any other District. ☐ There is a bankruptcy case concerning debtor's affiliate, general partner, or partnership pending in this District.

INFORMATION REGARDING DEBTOR (Check applicable boxes)

TYPE OF DEBTOR
☐ Individual
☐ Joint (Husband and Wife)
☐ Partnership
☐ Other _____

☐ Corporation Publicly Held
☐ Corporation Not Publicly Held
☐ Municipality

NATURE OF DEBT
☐ Non-Business/Consumer   ☐ Business - Complete A & B below

A. TYPE OF BUSINESS (Check one)
☐ Farming
☐ Professional
☐ Retail/Wholesale
☐ Railroad
☐ Transportation
☐ Manufacturing/Mining
☐ Stockbroker
☐ Commodity Broker
☐ Construction
☐ Real Estate
☐ Other Business

B. BRIEFLY DESCRIBE NATURE OF BUSINESS

CHAPTER OR SECTION OF BANKRUPTCY CODE UNDER WHICH THE PETITION IS FILED (Check one box)
☐ Chapter 7   ☐ Chapter 11   ☐ Chapter 13
☐ Chapter 9   ☐ Chapter 12   ☐ Sec. 304 - Case Ancilary to Foreign Processing

FILING FEE (Check one box)
☐ Filing fee attached
☐ Filing fee to be paid in installments. (Applicable to individuals only.) Must attach signed application for the court's consideration certifying that the debtor is unable to pay fee except in installments. Rule 1006(b). See Official Form No. 3

NAME AND ADDRESS OF LAW FIRM OR ATTORNEY OR DEBTOR IN PRO SE

Telephone No.

NAME(S) OF ATTORNEY(S) DESIGNATED TO REPRESENT DEBTOR
(Print or Type Names)

☐ Debtor is not represented by an attorney

STATISTICAL/ADMINISTRATIVE INFORMATION (U.S.C. § 604)
(Estimates only) (Check applicable boxes)

THIS SPACE FOR COURT USE ONLY

☐ Debtor estimates that funds will be available for distribution to unsecured creditors.

☐ Debtor estimates that, after any exempt property is excluded and administrative expenses paid, there will be no funds available for distribution to unsecured creditors.

ESTIMATED NUMBER OF CREDITORS

1-15	16-49	50-99	100-199	200-999	1000-over
☐	☐	☐	☐	☐	☐

ESTIMATED ASSETS (In thousands of dollars)

Under 50	50-99	100-499	500-999	1000-9999	10,000-99,000	100,000-over
☐	☐	☐	☐	☐	☐	☐

ESTIMATED LIABILITIES (In thousands of dollars)

Under 50	50-99	100-499	500-999	1000-9999	10,000-99,000	100,000-over
☐	☐	☐	☐	☐	☐	☐

EST. NO. OF EMPLOYEES - CH. 11 & 12 ONLY

0	1-19	20-99	100-999	1000-over
☐	☐	☐	☐	☐

EST. NO. OF EQUITY SECURITY HOLDERS - CH. 11 & 12 ONLY

0	1-19	20-99	100-499	500-over
☐	☐	☐	☐	☐

WOLCOTTS FORM B1p1

Name of Debtor _____

Case No _____

FILING OF PLAN	
For Chapter 9, 11, 12 and 13 cases only. Check appropriate box.	
☐ A copy of debtor's proposed plan dated _____ is attached	☐ Debtor intends to file a plan within the time allowed by statute, rule of order of the court

PRIOR BANKRUPTCY CASE FILED WITHIN LAST 6 YEARS (If more than one, attach additional sheet)		
Location Where Filed	Case Number	Date Filed

PENDING BANKRUPTCY CASE FILED BY ANY SPOUSE, PARTNER, OR AFFILIATE OF THE DEBTOR (If more than one, attach additional sheet)		
Name of Debtor	Case Number	Date
Relationship	District	Judge

REQUEST FOR RELIEF

Debtor requests relief in accordance with the chapter of title 11, United States Code specified in this petition

SIGNATURES

ATTORNEY

X_____   _____
Signature   Date

INDIVIDUAL JOINT DEBTOR(S)	CORPORATE OR PARTNERSHIP DEBTOR
I declare under penalty of perjury that the information provided in this petition is true and correct	I declare under penalty of perjury that the information provided in this petition is true and correct and that the filing of this petition on behalf of the debtor has been authorized
X_____ Signature of Debtor	X_____ Signature of Authorized Individual
Date _____	_____ Print or Type Name of Authorized Individual
X_____ Signature of Joint Debtor	_____ Title of Individual Authorized by Debtor to File this Petition
Date _____	Date _____

EXHIBIT "A" (To be completed if debtor is a corporation, requesting relief under Chapter 11.)

☐ Exhibit "A" is attached and made a part of this petition

TO BE COMPLETED BY INDIVIDUAL CHAPTER 7 DEBTOR WITH PRIMARILY CONSUMER DEBTS (See P.L. 98-353 § 322)

I am aware that I may proceed under chapter 7, 11, or 12 of title 11, United States Code, understand the relief available under such chapter, and choose to proceed under chapter 7 of such title

If I am represented by an attorney Exhibit B has been completed

X_____   _____
Signature of Debtor   Date

X_____   _____
Signature of Joint Debtor   Date

EXHIBIT "B" (To be completed by attorney for individual chapter 7 debtor(s) with primarily consumer debts.)

I, the attorney for the debtor(s) named in the foregoing petition, declare that I have informed the debtor(s) that (he, she, or they) may proceed under chapter 7, 11, 12, or 13 of title 11, United States Code, and have explained the relief available under such chapter.

X_____   _____
Signature of Attorney   Date

WOLCOTTS FORM B1p2

4

FORM 4.2

Schedules of Assets and Liabilities

FORM B6 - Cont.
(6/90)

United States Bankruptcy Court

_____ District of _____

In re _____, Case No. _____
                     Debtor   (If known)

SUMMARY OF SCHEDULES

Indicate as to each schedule whether that schedule is attached and state the number of pages in each. Report the totals from Schedules A, B, D, E, F, I, and J in the boxes provided. Add the amounts from Schedules A and B to determine the total amount of the debtor's assets. Add the amounts from Schedules D, E, and F to determine the total amount of the debtor's liabilities.

NAME OF SCHEDULE	ATTACHED (YES/NO)	NO. OF SHEETS	AMOUNTS SCHEDULED		
			ASSETS	LIABILITIES	OTHER
A - Real Property			$		
B - Personal Property			$		
C - Property Claimed As Exempt					
D - Creditors Holding Secured Claims				$	
E - Creditors Holding Unsecured Priority Claims				$	
F - Creditors Holding Unsecured Nonproperty Claims				$	
G - Executory Contracts and Unexpired Leases					
H - Codebtors					
I - Current Income of Individual Debtor(s)					$
J - Current Expenditures of Individual Debtor(s)					$
Total Number of sheets in ALL Schedules ▶					
Total Assets ▶			$		
Total Liabilities ▶				$	

WOLCOTTS FORM B6p2

FORM B6A
(10/89)

In re _____ .   Case No. _____
                        Debtor   (If known)

SCHEDULE A - REAL PROPERTY

Except as directed below, list all real property in which the debtor has any legal, equitable, or future interest, including all property owned as a co-tenant, community property, or in which the debtor has a life estate. Include any property in which the debtor holds rights and powers exercisable for the debtor's own benefit. If the debtor is married, state whether husband, wife, or both own the property by placing an "H," "W," "J," or "C" in the column labeled "Husband, Wife, Joint, or Community)." If the debtor holds no interest in real property, write "None" under "Description and Location of Property."

Do not include interests in executory contracts and unexpired leases on this schedule. List them in Schedule G - Executory Contracts and Unexpired Leases.

If an entity claims to have a lien or hold a secured interest in any property, state the amount of the secured claim. See Schedule D. If no entity claims to hold a secured interest in the property, write "None" in the column labeled "Amount of Secured Claim."

If the debtor is an individual or if a joint petition is filed, state the amount of any exemption claimed in the property only in Schedule C - Property Claimed as Exempt.

DESCRIPTION AND LOCATION OF PROPERTY	NATURE OF DEBTOR'S INTEREST IN PROPERTY	HUSBAND, WIFE, JOINT OR COMMUNITY	CURRENT MARKET VALUE OF DEBTOR'S INTEREST IN PROPERTY WITHOUT DEDUCTING ANY SECURED CLAIM OR EXEMPTION	AMOUNT OF SECURED CLAIM

Total ▶ $ _____

(Report also on Summary of Schedules.)

WOLCOTTS FORM B6A

8

FORM B6B
(10/89)

In re _____ .   Case No. _____
                          Debtor   (If known)

SCHEDULE B - PERSONAL PROPERTY

Except as directed below, list all personal property of the debtor of whatever kind. If the debtor has no property in one or more of the categories, place an "X" in the appropriate position in the column labeled "None." If additional space is needed in any category, attach a separate sheet properly identified with the case name, case number, and the number of the category. If the debtor is married, state whether husband, wife, or both own the property by placing an "H," "W," "J," or "C" in the column labeled "Husband, Wife, Joint, or Community." If the debtor is an individual or a joint petition is filed, state the amount of any exemptions claimed only in Schedule C - Property Claimed as Exempt.

Do not list interests in executory contracts and unexpired leases on this schedule. List them in Schedule G - Executory Contracts and Unexpired Leases.

If the property is being held for the debtor by someone else, state that person's name and address under "Description and Location of Property."

TYPE OF PROPERTY	NONE	DESCRIPTION AND LOCATION OF PROPERTY	HUSBAND, WIFE, JOINT COMMUNITY	CURRENT MARKET VALUE OF DEBTOR'S INTEREST IN PROPERTY, WITHOUT DEDUCTING ANY SECURED CLAIM OR EXEMPTION
1. Cash on hand.				
2. Checking, savings or other financial accounts, certificates of deposit, or shares in banks, savings and loan, thrift, building and loan, and homestead associations, or credit unions, brokerage houses, or cooperatives.				
3. Security deposits with public utilities, telephone companies, landlords, and others.				
4. Household goods and furnishings, including audio, video, and computer equipment.				
5. Books, pictures and other art objects, antiques, stamp, coin, record, tape, compact disc, and other collections or collectibles.				
6. Wearing apparel.				
7. Furs and jewelry.				
8. Firearms and sports, photographic, and other hobby equipment.				
9. Interests in insurance policies. Name insurance company of each policy and itemize surrender or refund value of each.				
10. Annuities. Itemize and name each issuer.				

WOLCOTTS FORM B6Bp1

9

In re _____ .   Case No. _____
                    Debtor   (If known)

SCHEDULE B - PERSONAL PROPERTY
(Continuation Sheet)

TYPE OF PROPERTY	NONE	DESCRIPTION AND LOCATION OF PROPERTY	HUSBAND, WIFE, JOINT COMMUNITY	CURRENT MARKET VALUE OF DEBTOR'S INTEREST IN PROPERTY, WITH-OUT DEDUCTING ANY SECURED CLAIM OR EXEMPTION
11. Interests in IRA, ERISA, Keogh, or other pension or profit sharing plans. Itemize.				
12. Stock and interests in incorporated and unincorporated businesses. Itemize.				
13. Interests in partnerships or joint ventures. Itemize.				
14. Government and corporate bonds and other negotiable and non-negotiable instruments.				
15. Accounts Receivable.				
16. Alimony, maintenance, support, and property settlements to which the debtor is or may be entitled. Give particulars.				
17. Other liquidated debts owing debtor include tax refunds. Give particulars.				
18. Equitable or future interests, life estates, and rights or powers exercisable for the benefit of the debtor other than those listed in Schedule of Real Property.				
19. Contingent and non-contingent interests in estate of a decedent, death benefit plan, life insurance policy, or trust.				
20. Other contingent and unliquidated claims of every nature, including tax refunds, counterclaims of the debtor, and rights to setoff claims. Give estimated value of each.				
21. Patents, coprights, and other intellectual property. Give particulars.				
22. Licenses, franchises, and other general intangibles. Give particulars.				

WOLCOTTS FORM B6Bp2

10

In re _____ .   Case No. _____
                              Debtor   (If known)

SCHEDULE B - PERSONAL PROPERTY
(Continuation Sheet)

TYPE OF PROPERTY	NONE	DESCRIPTION AND LOCATION OF PROPERTY	HUSBAND, WIFE, JOINT COMMUNITY	CURRENT MARKET VALUE OF DEBTOR'S INTEREST IN PROPERTY, WITH-OUT DEDUCTING ANY SECURED CLAIM OR EXEMPTION
23. Automobiles, trucks, trailers, and other vehicles.				
24. Boats, motort, and accessories.				
25. Aircraft and accessories				
26. Office equipment, furnishings, and supplies.				
27. Mahinery, fixtures, equipment and supplies used in business.				
28. Inventory.				
29. Animals.				
30. Crops - growing or harvested. Give particulars.				
31. Framing equipment and implements.				
32. Farm supplies, chemicals, and feed.				
33. Other personal property of any kind not already listed. Itemize.				

_____ continuation sheets attached   Total → $ _____

(Include amounts from any continuation sheets attached. Report total also on Summary of Schedules.)

WOLCOTTS FORM B6Bp3

11

FORM B6C
(6/90)

In re _____ .   Case No. _____
                  Debtor   (If known)

SCHEDULE C - PROPERTY CLAIMED AS EXEMPT

Debtor elects the exemption to which debtor is entitled under

(Check one box)

☐ 11 U.S.C. § 522(b)(1) Exemptions provided in 11 U.S.C. § 522(d). Note: These exemptions are available only in certain states.

☐ 11 U.S.C. § 522(b)(2) Exemptions available under applicable nonbankruptcy federal laws, state or local law where the debtor's domicile has been located for the 180 days immediately preceding the filing of the petition, or for a longer portion of the 180-day period than in any other place, and the debtor's interest as a tenant by the entirety or joint tenant to the extent the interest is exempt from process under applicable nonbankruptcy law.

DESCRIPTION OF PROPERTY	SPECIFY LAW PROVIDING EACH EXEMPTION	VALUE OF CLAIMED EXEMPTION	CURRENT MARKET VALUE OF PROPERTY WITHOUT DEDUCTING EXEMPTIONS

WOLCOTTS FORM B6C

FORM B6D
(6/90)

In re _____ .   Case No. _____
          Debtor   (If known)

SCHEDULE D - CREDITORS HOLDING SECURED CLAIMS

State the name, mailing address, including zip code, and account number, if any, of all entities holding claims secured by property of the debtor as of the date of filing of the petition. List creditors holding all types of secured interests such as judgment liens, garnishments, statutory liens, mortgages, deeds of trust, and other security interests. List creditors in alphabetical order to the extent practicable. If all secured creditors will not fit on this page, use the continuation sheet provided.

If any entity other than a spouse in a joint case may be jointly liable on a claim, place an "X" in the column labeled "Codebtor," include the entity on the appropriate schedule of creditors, and complete Schedule H - Codebtors. If a joint petition is filed, state whether husband, wife, both of them, or the marital community may be liable on each claim by placing an "H," "W," "J," or "C" in the column labeled "Husband, Wife, Joint, or Community."

If the claim is contingent, place an "X" in the column labeled "Contingent." If the claim is unliquidated, place an "X" in the column labeled "Unliquidated." If the claim is disputed, place an "X" in the column labeled "Disputed." (You may need to place an "X" in more than one of these three columns.)

Report the total of all claims listed on this schedule in the box labeled "Total" on the last sheet of the completed schedule. Report this total also on the Summary of Schedules.

☐ Check this box if debtor has no creditors holding secured claims to report on this Schedule D.

CREDITOR'S NAME AND MAILING ADDRESS INCLUDING ZIP CODE	CODEBTOR	HUSBAND, WIFE, JOINT OR COMMUNITY	DATE CLAIM WAS INCURRED, NATURE OF LIEN, AND DESCRIPTION AND MARKET VALUE OF PROPERTY SUBJECT TO LIEN	CONTINGENT	UNLIQUIDATED	DISPUTED	AMOUNT OF CLAIM WITHOUT DEDUCTING VALUE OF COLLATERAL	UNSECURED PORTION, IF ANY
ACCOUNT NO.								
			Value $					
ACCOUNT NO.								
			Value $					
ACCOUNT NO.								
			Value $					
ACCOUNT NO.								
			Value $					

_____ Continuation sheets attached

Subtotal ➤ $
(Total of this page)

Total ➤ $
(Use only on last page)

WOLCOTTS FORM B6Dp1

(Report total also on Summary of Schedules)

13

FORM B6D - Cont.
(10/89)

In re _____ . Case No. _____
                              Debtor   (If known)

SCHEDULE D - CREDITORS HOLDING SECURED CLAIMS
(Continuation Sheet)

CREDITOR'S NAME AND MAILING ADDRESS INCLUDING ZIP CODE	CODEBTOR	HUSBAND, WIFE, JOINT OR COMMUNITY	DATE CLAIM WAS INCURRED, NATURE OF LIEN, AND DESCRIPTION AND MARKET VALUE OF PROPERTY SUBJECT TO LIEN	CONTINGENT	UNLIQUIDATED	DISPUTED	AMOUNT OF CLAIM WITHOUT DEDUCTING VALUE OF COLLATERAL	UNSECURED PORTION, IF ANY
ACCOUNT NO.			VALUE $					
ACCOUNT NO.			VALUE $					
ACCOUNT NO.			VALUE $					
ACCOUNT NO.			VALUE $					
ACCOUNT NO.			VALUE $					

Sheet _____ of _____ continuation sheets attached to Schedule of Creditors Holding Unsecured Claims   Subtotal ► $

(Total of this page)
Total ► $
(Use only on last page)

(Report total also on Summary of Schedules)

WOLCOTTS FORM B6Dcont.

14

FORM B6E
(6/90)

In re _____ .   Case No. _____
                        Debtor   (If known)

SCHEDULE E - CREDITORS HOLDING UNSECURED PRIORITY CLAIMS

A complete list of claims entitled to property, listed separately by type of priority, is to be set forth on the sheets provided. Only holders of unsecured claims entitled to priority should be listed in this schedule. In the boxes provided on the attached sheets, state the name and mailing address, including zip code, and account number if any, of all entities holding priority claims against the debtor or the property of the debtor, as of the date of the filing of this petition.

If any entity other than a spouse in a joint case may be jointly liable on a claim, place an "X" in the column labeled "Codebtor," include the entity on the appropriate schedule of creditors, and complete Schedule H - Codebtors. If a joint petition is filed, state whether husband, wife, both of them, or the marital community may be liable on each claim by placing an "H," "W," "J," or "C" in the column labeled "Husband, Wife, Joint, or Community."

If the claim is contingent, place an "X" in the column labeled "Contingent." If the claim is unliquidated, place an "X" in the column labeled "Unliquidated." If the claim is disputed, place an "X" in the column labeled "Disputed." (You may need to place an "X" in more than one of these three columns.)

Report the total of claims listed on each sheet in the box labeled, "Subtotal" on each sheet. Report the total of all claims listed on this Schedule E in the box labeled "Total" on the last sheet of the completed schedule. Repeat this total also on the Summary of Schedules.

☐ Check this box if debtor has no creditors holding unsecured priority claims to report on this Schedule E.

TYPES OF PRIORITY

☐ **Extensions of credit in an involuntary case**

Claims arising in the ordinary course of the debtor's business or financial affairs after the commencement of the case but before the earlier of the appointment of a trustee or the order for relief. 11 U.S.C. § 507(a)(2).

☐ **Wages, salaries, and commissions**

Wages, salaries, and commissions, including vacation, severance, and sick leave pay owing to employees, up to a maximum of $2000 per employee, earned within 90 days immediately preceding the filing of the original petition, or the cessation of business, whichever occurred first, to the extent provided in 11 U.S.C. § 507(a)(3).

☐ **Contributions to employee benefit plans**

Money owed to employee benefit plans for services rendered within 180 days immediately preceding the filing of the original petition, or the cessation of business, whichever occurred first, to the extent provided in 11 U.S.C. § 507(a)(4).

☐ **Certain farmers and fishermen**

Claims of certain farmers and fishermen, up to a maximum of $2000 per farmer or fisherman, against the debtor, as provided in 11 U.S.C. § 507(a)(5).

☐ **Deposits by individuals**

Claims of individuals up to a maximum of $900 for deposits for the purchase, lease, or rental of property or services for personal, family, or household use, that were not delivered or provided. 11 U.S.C. § 507(a)(6).

☐ **Taxes and Other Certain Debts Owed to Governmental**

Taxes, customs duties, and penalties owing to federal, state, and local governmental units as set forth in 11 U.S.C. §507(a)(7).

WOLCOTTS FORM B6E:p1   _____ continuation sheets attached

In re _____. Case No. _____
                    Debtor   (If known)

SCHEDULE E - CREDITORS, HOLDING UNSECURED PRIORITY CLAIMS
(Continuation Sheet)

_____
TYPE OF PRIORITY

CREDITOR'S NAME AND MAILING ADDRESS INCLUDING ZIP CODE	CODEBTOR	HUSBAND, WIFE, JOINT OR COMMUNITY	DATE CLAIM WAS INCURRED AND CONSIDERATION FOR CLAIM	CONTINGENT	UNLIQUIDATED	DISPUTED	TOTAL AMOUNT OF CLAIM	AMOUNT ENTITLED TO PRIORITY
ACCOUNT NO.								
ACCOUNT NO.								
ACCOUNT NO.								
ACCOUNT NO.								
ACCOUNT NO.								

Sheet no. _____ of _____ sheets attached to Schedule of Creditors

Subtotal ► $ _____
(Total of this page)
Total ► $ _____
(Use only on last page of the completed Schedule E)

(Report total also on Summary of Schedules)

Form B6F
(10/89)

In re _____ .   Case No. _____

                 Debtor   (If Known)

SCHEDULE F - CREDITORS HOLDING UNSECURED NONPRIORITY CLAIMS

State the name, mailing address, including zip code, and account number, if any, of all entities holding unsecured claims without priority against the debtor or the property of the debtor, as of the date of filing of the petition. Do not include claims listed in Schedules D and E. If all creditors will not fit on this page, use the continuation sheet provided.

If any entity other than a spouse in a joint case may be jointly liable on a claim, place an "X" in the column labeled "Codebtor," include the entity on the appropriate schedule of creditors, and complete Schedule H - Codebtors. If a joint petition is filed, state whether husband, wife, both of them, or the marital community may be liable on each claim by placing an "H," "W," "J," or "C" in the column labeled "Husband, Wife, Joint, or Community."

If the claim is contingent, place an "X" in the column labeled "Contingent." If the claim is unliquidated, place an "X" in the column labeled "Unliquidated." If the claim is disputed, place an "X" in the column labeled "Disputed." (You may need to place an "X" in more than one of these three columns.)

Report total of all claims listed on this schedule in the box labeled "Total" on the last sheet of the completed schedule. Report this total also on the Summary of Schedules.

☐ Check this box if debtor has no creditors holding unsecured non priority claims to report on this Schedule F.

CREDITOR'S NAME AND MAILING ADDRESS INCLUDING ZIP CODE	CODEBTOR	HUSBAND, WIFE OR JOINT	DATE CLAIM WAS INCURRED AND CONSIDERATION FOR CLAIM. IF CLAIM IS SUBJECT TO SETOFF, SO STATE	CONTINGENT	UNLIQUIDATED	DISPUTED	AMOUNT OF CLAIM
ACCOUNT NO.							
ACCOUNT NO.							
ACCOUNT NO.							
ACCOUNT NO.							

_____ continuation sheets attached   Subtotal ➤ | $

                                                          Total ➤ | $

WOLCOTTS FORM B6Fp1

(Report total also on Summary of Schedules)

Form B6F
(10/89)

In re _____.   Case No. _____
                              Debtor   (If known)

SCHEDULE F - CREDITORS HOLDING UNSECURED NONPRIORITY
(Continuation Sheet)

CREDITOR'S NAME AND MAILING ADDRESS INCLUDING ZIP CODE	CODEBTOR	HUSBAND, WIFE OR JOINT	DATE CLAIM WAS INCURRED AND CONSIDERATION FOR CLAIM, IF CLAIM IS SUBJECT TO SETOFF, SO STATE	CONTINGENT	UNLIQUIDATED	DDISPUTED	AMOUNT OF CLAIM
ACCOUNT NO.							
ACCOUNT NO.							
ACCOUNT NO.							
ACCOUNT NO.							
ACCOUNT NO.							

Sheet no. _____ of _____ sheets attached to Schedule of
Creditors Holding Unsecured Nonpriority Claims

Subtotal ➤ $ _____
(Total of this page)
Total ➤ $ _____
(Use only on last page of the completed Schedule F)

WOLCOTTS FORM B6Fcont.

(Report total also on Summary of Schedules)

18

Form B6G
(10/89)

In re _____.   Case No. _____
                          Debtor   (If Known)

SCHEDULE G - EXECUTORY CONTRACTS AND UNEXPIRED LEASES

Describe all executory contracts of any nature and all unexpired leases of real or personal property. Include any timeshare interests.

State nature of debtor's interest in contract, i.e., "Purchaser," "Agent," etc. State whether debtor is the lessor or lessee of a lease.

Provide the names and complete mailing addresses of all other parties to each lease or contract described.

NOTE: A party listed on this schedule will not receive notice of the filing of this case unless the party is also scheduled in the appropriate schedule of creditors.

☐ Check this box if debtor has no executory contracts or unexpired leases.

NAME AND MAILING ADDRESS, INCLUDING ZIP CODE, OF OTHER PARTIES TO LEASE OR CONTRACT	DESCRIPTION OF CONTRACT OR LEASE AND NATURE OF DEBTOR'S INTEREST. STATE WHETHER LEASE IS FOR NONRESIDENTIAL REAL PROPERTY. STATE CONTRACT NUMBER OF ANY GOVERNMENT CONTRACT

WOLCOTTS FORM B6G

Form B6H
(6/90)

In re _____ .   Case No. _____
                    Debtor   (If known)

SCHEDULE H - CODEBTORS

Provide the information requested concerning any person or entity, other than a spouse in a joint case, that is also liable on any debts listed by debtor in the schedules of creditors. Include all guarantors and co-signers. In community property states, a married debtor not filing a joint case should report the name and address of the nondebtor spouse on this schedule. Include all names used by the nondebtor spouse during the six years immediately preceding the commencement of this case.

☐ Check this box if debtor has no codebtors.

NAME AND ADDRESS OF CODEBTOR	NAME AND ADDRESS OF CREDITOR

WOLCOTTS FORM B6H

20

Form B6I
(6/90)

In re _____ .   Case No. _____
                        Debtor   (If known)

SCHEDULE I - CURRENT INCOME OF INDIVIDUAL DEBTOR(S)

The column labeled "Spouse" must be completed in all cases filed by joint debtors and by a married debtor in a chapter 12 or 13 case whether or not a joint petition is filed, unless the spouses are separated and a joint petition is not filed.

Debtor's Marital Status:	DEPENDENTS OF DEBTOR AND SPOUSE			
	NAMES		AGE	RELATIONSHIP

EMPLOYMENT :	DEBTOR	SPOUSE
Occupation Name of Employer		
How long employed		
Address of Employer		

Income: (Estimate of average monthly income)	DEBTOR	SPOUSE
Current monthly gross wages, salary, and commissions (pro rate if not paid monthly.)	$_____	$_____
Estimated monthly overtime	$_____	$_____
SUBTOTAL	$_____	$_____
LESS PAYROLL DEDUCTIONS		
a. Payroll taxes and social security	$_____	$_____
b. Insurance	$_____	$_____
c. Union dues	$_____	$_____
d. Other (Specify _____)	$_____	$_____
SUBTOTAL OF PAYROLL DEDUCTIONS	$_____	$_____
TOTAL NET MONTHLY TAKE HOME PAY	$_____	$_____
Regular income from operation of business or profession or farm (attach detailed statement)	$_____	$_____
Income from real property	$_____	$_____
Interest and dividends	$_____	$_____
Alimony, maintenance or support payments payable to the debtor for the debtor's use or that of dependents listed above.	$_____	$_____
Social security or other government assistance (Specify) _____	$_____	$_____
Pension or retirement income	$_____	$_____
Other monthly income	$_____	$_____
(Specify) _____	$_____	$_____
_____	$_____	$_____
TOTAL MONTHLY INCOME	$_____	$_____

TOTAL COMBINED MONTHLY INCOME $_____   (Report also on Summary of Schedules)

Describe any increase or decrease of more than 10% in any of the above categories anticipated to occur within the year following the filing of this document:

WOLCOTTS FORM B6I

21

FORM B6J
(6/90)

In re _____ .   Case No. _____
                        Debtor   (If known)

SCHEDULE J - CURRENT EXPENDITURES OF INDIVIDUAL DEBTORS

Complete this schedule by estimating the average monthly expenses of the debtor and the debtor's family. Pro rate any payments made bi-weekly, quarterly, semi-annually, or annually to show monthly rate.

☐ Check this box if a joint petition is filed and debtor's spouse maintains a separate household. Complete a separate schedule of expenditures labeled "Spouse."

Rent or home mortgage payment (include lot rented for mobile home)	$ _____
Are real estate taxes included? Yes _____ No _____	
Is property insurance included? Yes _____ No _____	
Utilities Electricity and heating fuel	$ _____
Water and sewer	$ _____
Telephone	$ _____
Other _____	$ _____
Home Maintenance (Repairs and upkeep)	$ _____
Food	$ _____
Clothing	$ _____
Laundry and dry cleaning	$ _____
Medical and dental expenses	$ _____
Transportation (not including car payments)	$ _____
Recreation, clubs and entertainment, newspapers, magazines, etc.	$ _____
Charitable contributions	$ _____
Insurance (not deducted from wages or included in home mortgage payments)	
Homeowner's or renter's	$ _____
Life	$ _____
Health	$ _____
Auto	$ _____
Other _____	$ _____
Taxes (not deducted from wages or included in home mortgage payuments)	
(Specify) _____	$ _____
Installment payments (In chapter 12 and 13 cases, do not list payments to be included in the plan)	
Auto	$ _____
Other _____	$ _____
Other _____	$ _____
Alimony, maintenance, and support paid to others	$ _____
Payments for support of additional dependents not living at your home	$ _____
Regular expenses from operation of business, profession, or farm (attach detailed statement)	$ _____
Other _____	$ _____

TOTAL MONTHLY EXPENSES (Report also on Summary of Schedules) | $ _____ |

(FOR CHAPTER 12 DEBTORS ONLY)
Provide the information requested below, including whether plan payments are to be made bi-weekly, monthly, annually, or at some other regular interval.

A. Total projected monthly income	$ _____
B. Total projected monthly expenses	$ _____
C. Excess income (A minus B)	$ _____
D. Total amount to be paid into plan each _____	$ _____
(interval)	

WOLCOTTS FORM B6J

22

FORM B6 - Cont.
(6/90)

In re _____ .   Case No. _____
                          Debtor   (If known)

DECLARATION CONCERNING DEBTOR'S SCHEDULES

DECLARATION UNDER PENALTY OF PERJURY BY INDIVIDUAL DEBTOR

I declare under penalty of perjury that I have read the foregoing summary and schedules, consisting of _____ sheets,
and that they are true and correct to the best of my knowledge, information, and belief.   (Total shown on summary page plus 1)

Date _____   Signature _____
                                                                                    Debtor

Date _____   Signature _____
                                                                            (Joint Debtor, if any)

                                                          [If joint case, both spouses must sign]

- -

DECLARATION UNDER PENALTY OF PERJURY ON BEHALF OF CORPORATION OR PARTNERSHIP

I, the _____ [the president or other officer or an authorized agent of the corporation or a member or an
authorized agent of the partnership] of the _____ [corporation or partnership] named as debtor in this case,
declare under penalty of perjury that I have read the following summary and schedules, consisting of _____ sheets, and that
they are true and correct to the best of my knowledge, information, and belief.   (Total shown on summary page plus 1)

Date _____   Signature _____

                                                                    _____
                                                                    [Print or type name of individual signing on behalf of debtor]

[An individual signing on behalf of a partnership or corporation must indicate position or relationship to debtor.]

- -

Penalty for making a false statement or concealing property. Fine of up to $500,000 or imprisonment for up to 5 years or both. 18 U.S.C. §§ 152 and 3571.

WOLCOTTS FORM B6DECL

23

FORM 4.3

Statement of Financial Affairs

FORM 7. STATEMENT OF FINANCIAL AFFAIRS

UNITED STATES BANKRUPTCY COURT
_____ District of _____

In Re: _____ .   Case No._____
            (Name)   (If Known)
              Debtor

STATEMENT OF FINANCIAL AFFAIRS

This statement is to be completed by every debtor. Spouses filing a joint petition may file a single statement on which the information for both spouses is combined. If the case is filed under chapter 12 or chapter 13, a married debtor must furnish information for both spouses whether or not a joint petition is filed, unless the spouses are separated and a joint petition is not filed. An individual debtor engaged in business as a sole proprietor, partner, family farmer, or self-employed professional, should provide the information requested on this statement concerning all such activities as well as the individual's personal affairs.

Questions 1 - 15 are to be completed by all debtors. Debtors that are or have been in business, as defined below, also must complete Questions 16 - 21. **Each question must be answered. If the answer to any question is "None," or the question is not applicable, mark the box labeled "None."** If additional space is needed for the answer to any question, use and attach a separate sheet properly identified with the case name, case number (if known), and the number of the question.

DEFINITIONS

"In business." A debtor is "in business" for the purpose of this form if the debtor is a corporation or partnership. An individual debtor is "in business" for the purpose of this form if the debtor is or has been, within the two years immediately preceding the filing of the this bankruptcy case, any of the following: an officer, director, managing executive, or person in control of a corporation; a partner, other than a limited partner, of a partnership; a sole proprietor or self-employed.

"Insider." The term "insider" includes but is not limited to: relatives of the debtor; general partners of the debtor and their relatives; corporations of which the debtor is an officer, director, or person in control; officers, directors, and any person in control of a corporate debtor and their relatives; affiliates of the debtor and insiders of such affiliates; any managing agent of the debtor. 11 U.S.C. § 101(30).

---

1. Income from employment or operation of business

None
☐

State the gross amount of income the debtor has received from employment, trade, or profession, or from operation of the debtor's business from the beginning of this calendar year to the date this case was commenced. State also the gross amounts received during the **two years** immediately preceding this calendar year. (A debtor that maintains, or has maintained, financial records on the basis of a fiscal rather than a calendar year may report fiscal year income. Identify the beginning and ending dates of the debtor's fiscal year.) If a joint petition is filed, state income for each spouse separately. (Married debtors filing under chapter 12 or chapter 13 must state income of both spouses whether or not a joint petition is filed, unless the spouses are separated and a joint petition is not filed.)

AMOUNT   SOURCE (if more than one)

2. Income other than from employment or operation of business

None State the amount of income received by the debtor other than from employment, trade,
☐ profession, or operation of the debtor's business during the **two years** immediately preceding the
commencement of this case. Give particulars. If a joint petition is filed, state income for each spouse
separately. (Married debtors filing under chapter 12 or chapter 13 must state income for each spouse
whether or not a joint petition is filed, unless the spouses are separated and a joint petition is not filed.)

AMOUNT   SOURCE

---

3. Payments to creditors

None a. List all payments on loans, installment purchases of goods or services, and other debts,
☐ aggregating more than $600 to any creditor, made within **90 days** immediately preceding the
commencement of this case. (Married debtors filing under chapter 12 or chapter 13 must include
payments by either or both spouses whether or not a joint petition is filed, unless the spouses are
separated and a joint petition is not filed.)

NAME AND ADDRESS OF CREDITOR	DATES OF PAYMENTS	AMOUNT PAID	AMOUNT STILL OWING

None b. List all payments made within **one year** immediately preceding the commencement of this case
☐ to or for the benefit of creditors who are or were insiders. (Married debtors filing under chapter 12 or
chapter 13 must include payments by either or both spouses whether or not a joint petition is filed,
unless the spouses are separated and a joint petition is not filed.)

NAME AND ADDRESS OF CREDITOR AND RELATIONSHIP TO DEBTOR	DATE OF PAYMENT	AMOUNT PAID	AMOUNT STILL OWING

---

4. Suits, executions, garnishments and attachments

None a. List all suits to which the debtor is or was a party within **one year** immediately preceding the filing
☐ of this bankruptcy case. (Married debtors filing under chapter 12 or chapter 13 must include
information concerning either or both spouses whether or not a joint petition is filed, unless the
spouses are separated and a joint petition is not filed.)

CAPTION OF SUIT AND CASE NUMBER	NATURE OF PROCEEDING	COURT AND LOCATION	STATUS OR DISPOSITION

WOLCOTTS FORM B7p2

28

None   b.   Describe all property that has been attached, garnished or seized under any legal or equitable
☐   process within **one year** immediately preceding the commencement of this case. (Married debtors filing under chapter 12 or chapter 13 must include information concerning property of either or both spouses whether or not a joint petition is filed, unless the spouses are separated and a joint petition is not filed.)

NAME AND ADDRESS OF PERSON FOR WHOSE BENEFIT PROPERTY WAS SEIZED	DATE OF SEIZURE	DESCRIPTION AND VALUE OF PROPERTY

_____

5. Repossessions, foreclosures and returns

None   List all property that has been repossessed by a creditor, sold at a foreclosure sale, transferred
☐   through a deed in lieu of foreclosure or returned to the seller, within **one year** immediately preceding the commencement of this case. (Married debtors filing under chapter 12 or chapter 13 must include information concerning property of either or both spouses whether or not a joint petition is filed, unless the spouses are separated and a joint petition is not filed.)

NAME AND ADDRESS OF CREDITOR OR SELLER	DATE OF REPOSSESSION, FORECLOSURE SALE, TRANSFER OR RETURN	DESCRIPTION AND VALUE OF PROPERTY

_____

6. Assignments and receiverships

None   a.   Describe any assignment of property for the benefit of creditors made within **120 days** immediately
☐   preceding the commencement of this case. (Married debtors filing under chapter 12 or chapter 13 must include any assignment by either or both spouses whether or not a joint petition is filed, unless the spouses are separated and a joint petition is not filed.)

NAME AND ADDRESS OF ASSIGNEE	DATE OF ASSIGNMENT	TERMS OF ASSIGNMENT OR SETTLEMENT

_____

None   b.   List all property which has been in the hands of a custodian, receiver, or court-appointed official
☐   within **one year** immediately preceding the commencement of this case. (Married debtors filing under chapter 12 or chapter 13 must include information concerning property of either or both spouses whether or not a joint petition is filed, unless the spouses are separated and a joint petition is not filed.)

NAME AND ADDRESS OF CUSTODIAN	NAME AND LOCATION OF COURT CASE TITLE & NUMBER	DATE OF ORDER	DESCRIPTION AND VALUE OF PROPERTY

WOLCOTTS FORM 117p3

7. Gifts

None
☐

List all gifts or charitable contributions made within **one year** immediately preceding the commencement of this case except ordinary and usual gifts to family members aggregating less than $200 in value per individual family member and charitable contributions aggregating less than $100 per recipient. (Married debtors filing under chapter 12 or chapter 13 must include gifts or contributions by either or both spouses whether or not a joint petition is filed, unless the spouses are separated and a joint petition is not filed.)

NAME AND ADDRESS OF PERSON OR ORGANIZATION	RELATIONSHIP TO DEBTOR, IF ANY	DATE OF GIFT	DESCRIPTION AND VALUE OF GIFT

8. Losses

None
☐

List all losses from fire, theft, other casualty or gambling within **one year** immediately preceding the commencement of this case **or since the commencement of this case.** (Married debtors filing under chapter 12 or chapter 13 must include losses by either or both spouses whether or not a joint petition is filed, unless the spouses are separated and a joint petition is not filed.)

DESCRIPTION AND VALUE OF PROPERTY	DESCRIPTION OF CIRCUMSTANCES AND, IF LOSS WAS COVERED IN WHOLE OR IN PART BY INSURANCE, GIVE PARTICULARS	DATE OF LOSS

9. Payments related to debt counseling or bankruptcy

None
☐

List all payments made or property transferred by or on behalf of the debtor to any persons, including attorneys, for consultation concerning debt consolidation, relief under the bankruptcy law or preparation of a petition in bankruptcy within **one year** immediately preceding the commencement of this case.

NAME AND ADDRESS OF PAYEE	DATE OF PAYMENT, NAME OF PAYOR IF OTHER THAN DEBTOR	AMOUNT OF MONEY OR DESCRIPTION AND VALUE OF PROPERTY

WOLCOTTS FORM B7p4

10. Other transfers

None ☐ a. List all other property, other than property transferred in the ordinary course of the business or financial affairs of the debtor, transferred either absolutely or as security within **one year** immediately preceding the commencement of this case. (Married debtors filing under chapter 12 or chapter 13 must include transfers by either or both spouses whether or not a joint petition is filed, unless the spouses are separated and a joint petition is not filed.)

NAME AND ADDRESS OF TRANSFEREE, RELATIONSHIP TO DEBTOR	DATE	DESCRIBE PROPERTY TRANSFERRED AND VALUE RECEIVED

---

11. Closed financial accounts

None ☐ List all financial accounts and instruments held in the name of the debtor or for the benefit of the debtor which were closed, sold, or otherwise transferred within **one year** immediately preceding the commencement of this case. Include checking, savings, or other financial accounts, certificates of deposit, or other instruments; shares and share accounts held in banks, credit unions, pension funds, cooperatives, associations, brokerage houses and other financial institutions. (Married debtors filing under chapter 12 or chapter 13 must include information concerning accounts or instruments held by or for either or both spouses whether or not a joint petition is filed, unless the spouses are separated and a joint petition is not filed.)

NAME AND ADDRESS OF INSTITUTION	TYPE AND NUMBER OF ACCOUNT AND AMOUNT OF FINAL BALANCE	AMOUNT AND DATE OF SALE OR CLOSING

---

12. Safe deposit boxes

None ☐ List each safe deposit or other box or depository in which the debtor has or had securities, cash, or other valuables within **one year** immediately preceding the commencement of this case. (Married debtors filing under chapter 12 or chapter 13 must include boxes or depositories of either or both spouses whether or not a joint petition is filed, unless the spouses are separated and a joint petition is not filed.)

NAME AND ADDRESS OF BANK OR OTHER DEPOSITORY	NAMES AND ADDRESSES OF THOSE WITH ACCESS TO BOX OR DEPOSITORY	DESCRIPTION OF CONTENTS	DATE OF TRANSFER OR SURRENDER, IF ANY

WOLCOTTS FORM B7p5

31

13. Setoffs

None   List all setoffs made by any creditor, including a bank, against a debt or deposit of the debtor
☐   within **90 days** preceding the commencement of this case. (Married debtors filing under chapter 12 or chapter 13 must include information concerning either or both spouses whether or not a joint petition is filed, unless the spouses are separated and a joint petition is not filed.)

NAME AND ADDRESS OF CREDITOR	DATE OF SETOFF	AMOUNT OF SETOFF

---

14. Property held for another person

None   List all property owned by another person that the debtor holds or controls.
☐

NAME AND ADDRESS OF OWNER	DESCRIPTION AND VALUE OF PROPERTY	LOCATION OF PROPERTY

---

15. Prior address of debtor

None   If the debtor has moved within the **two years** immediately preceding the commencement of this
☐   case, list all premises which the debtor occupied during that period and vacated prior to the commencement of this case. If a joint petition is filed, report also any separate address of either spouse.

ADDRESS	NAME USED	DATES OF OCCUPANCY

WOLCOTTS FORM B7p6

The following questions are to be completed by every debtor that is a corporation or partnership and by any individual debtor who is or has been, within the two years immediately preceding the commencement of this case, any of the following: an officer, director, managing executive, or owner of more than 5 percent of the voting securities of a corporation; a partner, other than a limited partner, of a partnership; a sole proprietor or otherwise self-employed.

(An individual or joint debtor should complete this portion of the statement only if the debtor is or has been in business, as defined above, within the two years immediately preceding the commencement of this case.)

16. Nature, location and name of business

None ☐   a. If the debtor is an individual, list the names and addresses of all businesses in which the debtor was an officer, director, partner, or managing executive of a corporation, partnership, sole proprietorship, or was a self-employed professional within the **two years** immediately preceding the commencement of this case, or in which the debtor owned 5 percent or more of the voting or equity securities within the two years immediately preceding the commencement of this case.

b. If the debtor is a partnership, list the names and addresses of all businesses in which the debtor was a partner or owned 5 percent or more of the voting securities, within the **two years** immediately preceding the commencement of this case.

c. If the debtor is a corporation, list the names and addresses of all businesses in which the debtor was a partner or owned 5 percent or more of the voting securities within the **two years** immediately preceding the commencement of this case.

NAME	ADDRESS	NATURE OF BUSINESS	BEGINNING AND ENDING DATES OF OPERATION

_____

17. Books, records and financial statements

None ☐   a. List all bookkeepers and accountants who within the **six years** immediately preceding the filing of this bankruptcy case kept or supervised the keeping of books of account and records of the debtor.

NAME AND ADDRESS	DATES SERVICES RENDERED

_____

None ☐   b. List all firms or individuals who within the **two years** immediately preceding the filing of this bankruptcy case have audited the books of account and records, or prepared a financial statement of the debtor.

NAME	ADDRESS	DATES SERVICES RENDERED

WOLCOTTS FORM B7p6A

33

None   c. List all firms or individuals who at the time of the commencement of this case were in possession of
☐   the books of account and records of the debtor. If any of the books of account and records are not
available, explain.

NAME   ADDRESS

None   d. List all financial institutions, creditors and other parties, including mercantile and trade agencies, to
☐   whom a financial statement was issued within the **two years** immediately preceding the
commencement of this case by the debtor.

NAME AND ADDRESS   DATE ISSUED

---

18. Inventories

None   a. List the dates of the last two inventories taken of your property, the name of the person who
☐   supervised the taking of each inventory, and the dollar amount and basis of each inventory.

                                              DOLLAR AMOUNT OF INVENTORY
DATE OF INVENTORY   INVENTORY   SUPERVISOR   (Specify cost, market or other basis)

None   b. List the name and address of the person having possession of the records of each of the two
☐   inventories reported in a., above.

                                    NAME AND ADDRESSES OF CUSTODIAN
DATE OF INVENTORY   OF INVENTORY RECORDS

---

19. Current Partners, Officers, Directors and Shareholders

None   a. If the debtor is a partnership, list the nature and percentage of partnership interest of each member
☐   of the partnership.

NAME AND ADDRESS   NATURE OF INTEREST   PERCENTAGE OF INTEREST

34

None b. If the debtor is a corporation, list all officers and directors of the corporation, and each stockholder
☐ who directly or indirectly owns, controls, or holds 5 percent or more of the voting securities of the
corporation.

| | | NATURE AND PERCENTAGE |
| NAME AND ADDRESS | TITLE | OF STOCK OWNERSHIP |

---

20. Former partners, officers, directors and shareholders

None a. If the debtor is a partnership, list each member who withdrew from the partnership within **one year**
☐ year immediately preceding the commencement of this case.

| NAME | ADDRESS | DATE OF WITHDRAWAL |

None b. If the debtor is a corporation, list all officers, or directors whose relationship with the corporation
☐ terminated within **one year** immediately preceding the commencement of this case.

| NAME AND ADDRESS | TITLE | DATE OF TERMINATION |

---

21. Withdrawals from a partnership or distributions by a corporation

None If the debtor is a partnership or corporation, list all withdrawals or distributions credited or given
☐ to an insider, including compensation in any form, bonuses, loans, stock redemptions, options exercised
and any other perquisite during **one year** immediately preceding the commencement of this case.

| NAME & ADDRESS OF RECIPIENT, RELATIONSHIP TO DEBTOR | DATE AND PURPOSE OF WITHDRAWAL | AMOUNT OF MONEY OR DESCRIPTION AND VALUE OF PROPERTY |

[If completed by an individual or individual and spouse]

I declare under penalty of perjury that I have read the answers contained in the foregoing statement of financial affairs and any attachments thereto and that they are true and correct.

Date _____ Signature _____
                                 of Debtor

Date _____ Signature _____
                                 of Joint Debtor
                                 (if any)

* * * * * *

[If completed on behalf of a partnership or corporation]

I, declare under penalty of perjury that I have read the answers contained in the foregoing statement of financial affairs and any attachments thereto and that they are true and correct to the best of my knowledge, information and belief.

Date _____ Signature _____

                                 _____
                                 Print Name and Title

[An individual signing on behalf of a partnership or corporation must indicate position or relationship to debtor.]

_____ continuation sheets attached

Penalty for making a false statement: Fine of up to $500,000 or imprisonment for up to 5 years, or both. 18 U.S.C. § 152 and 3571

WOLCOTTS FORM B7p7

FORM 4.4

Attorney Fee Disclosure Statement

United States Bankruptcy Court

_____District of_____

In re

Bankruptcy Case No.

Debtor

DISCLOSURE OF COMPENSATION OF ATTORNEY FOR DEBTOR

1. Pursuant to 11 U.S.C. § 329(a) and Bankruptcy Rule 2016(b), I certify that I am the attorney for the above-named debtor(s) and that compensation paid to me within one year before the filing of the petition in bankruptcy, or agreed to be paid to me, for services rendered or to be rendered on behalf of the debtor(s) in contemplation of or in connection with the bankruptcy case is as follows:

For legal services, I have agreed to accept . . . . $_____

Prior to the filing of this statement I have received . . . . $_____

Balance Due . . . . $_____

2. The source of the compensation paid to me was:

   ☐ Debtor   ☐ Other (specify)

3. The source of compensation to be paid to me is:

   ☐ Debtor   ☐ Other (specify)

4. ☐ I have not agreed to share the above-disclosed compensation with any other person unless they are members and associates of my law firm.

   ☐ I have agreed to share the above-disclosed compensation with a person or persons who are not members or associates of my law firm. A copy of the agreement, together with a list of the names of the people sharing in the compensation, is attached.

5. In return for the above-disclosed fee, I have agreed to render legal service for all aspects of the bankruptcy case, including:

   a. Analysis of the debtor's financial situation, and rendering advice to the debtor in determining whether to file a petition in bankruptcy;

   b. Preparation and filing of any petition, schedules, statement of affairs and plan which may be required;

   c. Representation of the debtor at the meeting of creditors and confirmation hearing, and any adjourned hearings thereof;

39

DISCLOSURE OF COMPENSATION OF ATTORNEY FOR DEBTOR (Continued)

    d. Representation of the debtor in adversary proceedings and other contested bankruptcy matters;

    e. [Other provisions as needed] .

6. By agreement with the debtor(s), the above-disclosed fee does not include the following services:

CERTIFICATION

    I certify that the foregoing is a complete statement of any agreement or arrangement for payment to me for representation of the debtor(s) in this bankruptcy proceeding.

_____   _____
         Date   *Signature of Attorney*

                                         _____
                                          Name of law firm

FORM 4.5

Involuntary Petition

FORM 5. INVOLUNTARY PETITION

United States Bankruptcy Court District of _____	INVOLUNTARY PETITION

IN RE (Name of debtor - If individual, enter: Last, First, Middle)	ALL OTHER NAMES used by debtor in the last 6 years (Include married, maiden, and trade names)
SOC SEC./TAX I.D. NO. (If more than one, state all)	
STREET ADDRESS OF DEBTOR (No. and street, city, state, and zip code)	MAILING ADDRESS OF DEBTOR (If different from street address)

COUNTY OR RESIDENCE OR PRINCIPAL PLACE OF BUSINESS	

LOCATION OF PRINCIPAL ASSETS OF BUSINESS DEBTOR (If different from previously listed addresses)

CHAPTER OF BANKRUPTCY CODE UNDER WHICH PETITION IS FILED

☐ Chapter 7   ☐ Chapter 11

INFORMATION REGARDING DEBTOR (Check applicable boxes)

Petitioners believe

☐ Debts are primarily consumer debts

☐ Debts are primarily business debts (Complete sections A and B)

TYPE OF DEBTOR

☐ Individual

☐ Partnership

☐ Other _____

☐ Corporation Publicly Held

☐ Corporation Not Publicly Held

A. TYPE OF BUSINESS (Check one)

☐ Professional   ☐ Transportation   ☐ Commodity Broker

☐ Retail/Wholesale   ☐ Manufacturing/   ☐ Construction

☐ Railroad   Mining   ☐ Real Estate

                     ☐ Stockbroker   ☐ Other

B. BRIEFLY DESCRIBE NATURE OF BUSINESS

VENUE

☐ Debtor has been domiciled or has had a residence, principal place of business, or principal assets in the District for 180 days immediately preceding the date of this petition or for a longer part of such 180 days than in any other District.

☐ A bankruptcy case concerning debtor's affiliate, general partner or partnership is pending in this District.

PENDING BANKRUPTCY CASE FILED BY OR AGAINST ANY PARTNER
OR AFFILIATE OF THIS DEBTOR (Report information for any additional cases on attached sheets.)

Name of Debtor	Case Number	Date
Relationship	District	Judge

ALLEGATIONS (Check applicable boxes)	COURT USE ONLY

1. ☐ Petitioner(s) are eligible to file this petition pursuant to 11 U.S.C. §303(b).

2. ☐ The debtor is a person against whom an order for relief may be entered under title 11 of the United States Code.

3.a. ☐ The debtor is generally not paying such debtor's debts as they become due, unless such debts are the subject of a bona fide dispute;

or

b. ☐ Within 120 days preceding the filing of this petition, a custodian, other than a trustee, receiver, or agent appointed or authorized to take charge of less than substantially all of the property of the debtor for the purpose of enforcing a lien against such property, was appointed or took possession.

TRANSFER OF CLAIM

☐ Check this box if there has been a transfer of any claim against the debtor by or to any petitioner. Attach all documents evidencing the transfer and any statements that are required under Bankruptcy Rule 1003(a).

REQUEST FOR RELIEF

Petitioner(s) request that an order for relief be entered against the debtor under the chapter of title 11, United States Code, specified in this petition.

Petitioner(s) declare under penalty of perjury that the foregoing is true and correct according to the best of their knowledge, information, and belief.

X_____
Signature of Petitioner or Representative (State title)

Name of Petitioner _____

Name & Mailing
Address of Individual _____
Signing in Representative
Capacity   _____

X_____
Signature of Attorney

Name of Attorney Firm (If any) _____

Address _____

Telephone No. _____

X_____
Signature of Petitioner or Representative (State title)

Name of Petitioner _____

Name & Mailing
Address of Individual _____
Signing in Representative
Capacity   _____

X_____
Signature of Attorney

Name of Attorney Firm (If any) _____

Address _____

Telephone No. _____

X_____
Signature of Petitioner or Representative (State title)

Name of Petitioner _____

Name & Mailing
Address of Individual _____
Signing in Representative
Capacity   _____

X_____
Signature of Attorney

Name of Attorney Firm (If any) _____

Address _____

Telephone No. _____

PETITIONING CREDITORS

Name and Address of Petitioner	Nature of Claim	Amount of Claim
Name and Address of Petitioner	Nature of Claim	Amount of Claim
Name and Address of Petitioner	Nature of Claim	Amount of Claim
Note: If there are more than three petitioners, attach additional sheets with the statement under penalty of perjury, petitioner(s) signatures under the statement and the name(s) of attorney(s) and petitioning creditor information in the format above.		Total Amount of Petitioners' Claims

____ continuation sheets attached

FORM 5.1

Notice of Intended Action

CSD 1180 [6/01/93]
Name, Address, Telephone No. & I.D. No.

UNITED STATES BANKRUPTCY COURT
SOUTHERN DISTRICT OF CALIFORNIA
940 Front Street, Room 5-N-26, San Diego, California 92189-0020

In Re

BANKRUPTCY NO.

Tax I.D.#:

Social Security #:   Debtor.

NOTICE OF INTENDED ACTION AND OPPORTUNITY FOR HEARING

TO THE DEBTOR, ALL CREDITORS AND OTHER PARTIES IN INTEREST:

YOU ARE HEREBY NOTIFIED that_____,
(select one:)   [ ] the Trustee   [ ] United States Trustee   [ ] Debtor-in-Possession
[ ] Creditor herein, proposes to:

[ ]   Use, sell or lease the following property not in the ordinary course of business
       [include information as required by Federal Rule of Bankruptcy Procedure 2002(c)(1)][1];
       or

[ ]   Abandon the following property [description of property to be abandoned][1]; or

[ ]   Compromise or settle the following controversy [description of controversy to be
       settled and financial impact on estate as required by Bankruptcy Local Rule 9019]; or

[ ]   Seek allowance of compensation or remuneration to debtor as follows [specify the
       nature]; or

[ ]   Other [specify the nature of the matter]:

---

[1]NOTE TO TRUSTEES: This form may not be used to request the Court to notice this action for
any case filed or converted to a Chapter 7 <u>after</u> JANUARY 1, 1985. Please use CSD 2063, CSD
2064, or CSD 2065.

CSD 1180   [Continued on Page 2]

47

If you object to the proposed action:

1. **YOU ARE REQUIRED** to obtain a hearing date and time from the appropriate Courtroom Deputy for the judge assigned to your bankruptcy case. *If a Chapter 7, 11, or 12 case,* determine which deputy to call by looking at the Bankruptcy Case No. in the caption on Page 1 of this notice. If the case number is followed by the letter(s):

   - M - call (619) 557-6019 - DEPARTMENT ONE
   - A - call (619) 557-6594 - DEPARTMENT TWO
   - H - call (619) 557-6018 - DEPARTMENT THREE
   - B - call (619) 557-5157 - DEPARTMENT FOUR

   For ALL Chapter 13 cases, call (619) 557-5955.

2. **WITHIN TWENTY-EIGHT (28)[2] DAYS FROM THE DATE OF SERVICE OF THIS MOTION,** you are further required to serve a copy of your DECLARATION IN OPPOSITION TO MOTION and separate REQUEST AND NOTICE OF HEARING [Local Form CSD 1184[3]] upon the undersigned moving party, together with any opposing papers. The opposing declaration shall be signed and verified in the manner prescribed by Federal Rule of Bankruptcy Procedure 9011, and the declaration shall:

   a. identify the interest of the opposing party; and

   b. state, with particularity, the grounds for the opposition.

3. YOU MUST file the original and one copy of the Declaration and Request and Notice of Hearing with proof of service with the Clerk of the U.S. Bankruptcy Court at 940 Front Street, Room 5-N-26, San Diego, California 92189-0020, no later than the next business day following the date of service.

IF YOU FAIL TO SERVE YOUR "DECLARATION IN OPPOSITION TO INTENDED ACTION" AND "REQUEST AND NOTICE OF HEARING" within the 28-day[2] period provided by this notice, NO HEARING SHALL TAKE PLACE, you shall lose your opportunity for hearing, and the moving party may proceed to take the intended action.

DATE OF SERVICE:

[U.S. TRUSTEE]   [TRUSTEE]   [DEBTOR-IN-POSSESSION]
[Attorney for Moving Party]

---

[2]If you were served by mail, you have three (3) additional days to take the above-state actions.
[3]You may obtain Local Form CSD 1184 from the office of the Clerk of the U.S. Bankruptcy Court.

CSD 1180

FORM 7.1

Application for Appointment of Attorney

Attorneys for Debtor-in-possession

UNITED STATES BANKRUPTCY COURT

SOUTHERN DISTRICT OF CALIFORNIA

In re   )   CASE NO. 88-00155-M11
)
HAPPY KIDS DAY CARE CENTER,   )   APPLICATION FOR APPOINTMENT
)   OF ATTORNEY
        Debtor-In-Possession.   )
_____)

The Application of Happy Kids Day Care Center, Inc., Debtor-In-Possession herein respectfully represents:

1.   On or about September 23, 1988 Debtor filed a Petition for Relief in this Court pursuant to Chapter 11 of Title 11, United States Code. _____ has been acting as counsel for the Debtor since this date.

2.   The Debtor, as Debtor-In-Possession, wishes to employ the law firm of _____ as its counsel in these proceedings. The attorneys that will appear on behalf of the Debtor-In-possession are duly admitted to practice before this Court.

3.   Debtor selected the law firm of _____ because of its experience in rendering counseling to the Debtor with respect to its financial affairs, with respect to the filing of the present petition, and with respect to services as may be necessary for proper administration of this estate in the formulation of a Plan of Reorganization.

4.   Debtor is currently making every effort to analyze its financial condition and eliminate expenses where necessary. It is the Debtor's intent to formulate a Plan of Reorganization in the near future which will set up an equitable repayment schedule to all creditors.

5.   The reorganization plans of this Debtor may be extensive, an expertise in the bankruptcy field is necessary. Therefore, it is necessary to employ bankruptcy counsel experienced in bankruptcy law and in particular Chapter 11 Reorganization. Because _____ _____ expertise in the area of bankruptcy law and reorganization, the Debtor believes that they will be best suited for the purposes of carrying out the plans of the Debtor stated herein.

6.   To the best of the Debtor's knowledge the law firm of _____ and its attorneys have no connection with the Debtor, the creditors, or any other party in interest or their respective attorneys, and represent no interest adverse to the Debtor as Debtor-In-Possession or the estate in matters upon which they are to be engaged as counsel.

WHEREFORE, Debtor prays that he be authorized pursuant to 11 U.S.C. Section 327(a) and Bankruptcy Rule 2014, to employ and appoint _____ to represent him as Debtor-In-Possession in this proceeding, at the firms prevailing hourly rates for insolvency counseling and representation.

DATED:_____   _____
                                  HAPPY KIDS DAY CARE CENTER

FORM 7.2

Declaration of Disinterest

Attorneys for Debtor

UNITED STATES BANKRUPTCY COURT

Southern District of California

In re   )   CASE NO. 88-00155-M11

)

HAPPY KIDS DAY CARE CENTER,   )   DECLARATION OF DISINTEREST

)

    Debtor-In-Possession.   )

_____)

I, hereby declare:

1.   I am an attorney duly admitted to practice law in the State of _____ in the Bankruptcy Court for the District of _____. I am an associate in the law firm of ___ _____ with offices located at _____ _____.

2.   The law firm of _____ is not now, nor has it been, a stockholder of the Debtor. Said law firm is not now, nor has it been, a director, officer or employee of the Debtor or any underwriter of Debtor's securities. The law firm of _____ _____ and its attorneys do not represent any interest materially adverse to the Debtor, the estate or representative thereof, in the matters in which the law firm is to be engaged.

I declare under penalty of perjury that the foregoing is true and correct to the best of my knowledge. Executed this _____ day of _____ at _____.

_____

FORM 7.3

Order Authorizing Appointment of Attorney

Attorneys for Debtor

UNITED STATES BANKRUPTCY COURT

Southern District of California

In re)	CASE NO. 88-00155-M11
)	
HAPPY KIDS DAY CARE CENTER,)	ORDER AUTHORIZING
)	APPOINTMENT OF ATTORNEY
Debtor-In-Possession.)	
_____)	

Upon the Application of Happy Kids Day Care Center, Inc., the above-named Debtor-In-Possession, praying for authority to employ and appoint the law firm of _____ to represent it as Debtor-In-Possession herein pursuant to 11 U.S.C. Section 327(a) and Bankruptcy Rule 2014, and appearing that no notice of hearing on said Application would be given, and further appearing that the members of the law firm appearing on behalf of the Debtor are duly admitted to practice in this Court, and the Court being satisfied that the law firm of _____ represents no interest materially adverse to said Debtor-In-Possession herein or its estate in the matters upon which they are to be engaged, their employment is necessary and would be in the best interests of the estate;

IT IS HEREBY ORDERED that Happy Kids Day Care Center, Inc. as Debtor-In-Possession, be and hereby is authorized to employ the law firm of _____ to represent it as Debtor-In-

Possession in the within proceeding at their prevailing rates for insolvency counseling and representation subject to review and approval by the Bankruptcy Court prior to payment of any such fee.

DATED:_____   _____
                                          UNITED STATES BANKRUPTCY JUDGE

FORM 7.4

Notice of Fee Hearing

Attorneys for Debtor

UNITED STATES BANKRUPTCY COURT
District of Hoynes

In re	)	CASE NO.: 95-8888-Z11
	)	
JOHN SMITH,	)	NOTICE OF HEARING ON
	)	INTERIM APPLICATION FOR
	)	ALLOWANCE OF ATTORNEYS'
	)	FEES FOR SERVICES
	)	RENDERED FROM _____
	)	TO _____ AND
	)	FOR REIMBURSEMENT OF
	)	COSTS ADVANCED (11 U.S.C.
	)	Sections 330 and 331)
	)	
Debtor-in-Possession.	)	Date:
	)	Time:
_____	)	Dept:

NOTICE TO ALL CREDITORS AND OTHER PARTIES IN INTEREST AND TO THEIR ATTORNEYS OF RECORD:

NOTICE IS HEREBY GIVEN that a hearing will be had before the Honorable _____, Bankruptcy Judge, on _____ at _____ a/p.m. in Department _____, United States Bankruptcy Court, Fifth Floor, 940 Front Street, Carroll, Hoynes, for the purpose of considering and acting upon the following Application and to hear any objections thereto, transact such other business as may properly come before said hearing:

_____ INTERIM APPLICATION FOR ALLOWANCE OF ATTORNEYS' FEES AND COSTS FOR SERVICES RENDERED DEBTOR.

PAYEE	REASONS	AMOUNT
Doe & Roe	Attorneys' Fees	$
50 Maple Street	Costs Advanced	$
Suite 800	Retainer	$
Carroll, Hoynes 92101		
	Total Fees	$

NOTICE IS FURTHER GIVEN that the Application referred to herein is on file with the above-referenced Court and is hereby referred to for particulars. The Application is available for review during normal working hours at the Bankruptcy Court, Fifth Floor, United States Courthouse, 940 Front Street, Carroll, Hoynes.

NOTICE IS FURTHER GIVEN that the persons objecting, if any, to this Application shall file written objections as provided by Rule 220-8 of the Local Rules and serve the above-named attorneys with a copy of said written objections, not less than seven (7) days prior to the date of the hearing.

                              DOE & ROE

DATED:_____   By:_____

FORM 7.5

Fee Application

Attorneys for Debtor

UNITED STATES BANKRUPTCY COURT
District of Hoynes

In re	CASE NO. 94-6666-A7
)	
)	SECOND AND FINAL
MORGAN AVENUE PROPERTIES)	APPLICATION FOR ALLOWANCE
)	OF ATTORNEY'S FEES FOR
)	SERVICES RENDERED TO
)	ESTATE FROM JANUARY 26,
)	1995 THROUGH MARCH 29,
)	1 9 9 6 A N D F O R
)	REIMBURSEMENT OF COSTS
)	ADVANCED (11 U.S.C. §§
)	327(a), 330 and 331)
Debtor)	
)	DATE: June 12, 1996
_____)	TIME: 9:30 a.m.
	DEPT: 3
	JUDGE: SCHULMAN

TO UNITED STATES BANKRUPTCY JUDGE ROSE G. SCHULMAN:

The application of CALEM & AUSTIN(hereinafter "Applicant") for services rendered from January 26, 1996 through March 29, 1996 and for reimbursement of costs advanced respectfully represents as follows:

I

PRELIMINARY STATEMENT

Morgan Avenue Properties ("Morgan" or "Debtor") filed its Chapter 7 petition on September 25, 1994. The order appointing Calem & Austin as attorneys for Morgan was entered on December 21, 1994.

This is Applicant's second and final application for an award of fees and costs. Applicant has previously been awarded fees of Ten Thousand Dollars ($10,000.00) and costs of Five Hundred Eighty Nine Dollars and Twenty-Six Cents ($589.26). Applicant currently holds no retainer.

II

DESCRIPTION OF PROFESSIONAL SERVICES RENDERED

The following portion of the Fee Application will set forth a general description of the principal areas in which professional services have been rendered to the debtor. Detailed descriptions of the services rendered by the applicant and its associate attorneys and law clerks is set forth in detail in Exhibits A-1 through A-42 which are attached to this Application and incorporated herein by this reference as though set forth in full.

(A) GENERAL BACKGROUND

Morgan had been in the business of real estate trust deed financing over a ten (10) year period. The President and Chief Financial Officer of Morgan, Mr. Gary Morgan, built a large following of investors in trust deeds, initiated and serviced by Morgan. Mr. Morgan passed away in November, 1993. After the death of Mr. Morgan, the company's practice of obtaining new capital through loans from investors was no longer available, as the company's real estate license terminated on Mr. Morgan's death.

The major assets of Morgan were notes and trust deeds. These notes had been pledged for payment on loans made to Morgan. An extensive pre-petition review and analysis of Morgan's exposure relative to the collateralized notes and trust deeds was required. In light of the complex nature of this estate, the collateralized notes and trust deeds were presented to the Trustee in a clear, concise, straightforward manner. The notes and trust deeds were explained in detail in the schedules. A description of property which had been transferred within the twelve (12) months prior to filing of the petition was also explained in detail.

The efforts of counsel for the Debtor saved the Trustee and his counsel substantial time and effort in the liquidation of this estate by properly organizing and identifying the complex asset structure in advance of filing.

(B) SUMMARY OF SERVICES PERFORMED FROM
JANUARY 26, 1995 THROUGH MARCH 29, 1996

Due to the large creditor body, amendments to the schedules were deemed necessary throughout the proceeding. Counsel was required to appear at Superior Court fast track hearings in the case entitled Green v. Morgan Avenue Properties, et al, Case No.

522806. Counsel communicated with the Trustee relative to the administration of the estate and responded to numerous telephone calls and correspondence from creditors, including the State Franchise Tax Board. Counsel assisted BARSI, the party managing the cross-collateralized notes, in locating original trust deed documents. Counsel also sought abandonment by the Trustee of a 1988 Toyota.

(C) SUMMARY OF HOURLY RATES AND TIME

EXPENDED FROM JANUARY 26, 1995 THROUGH

MARCH 29, 1996

Attorney	Time Expended	Hourly Rate	Value of Services
Flora L. Calem	4.40	$175.00	$770.00
Lauren S. Austin	4.40	175.00	770.00
Holly Geulbaum	1.10	150.00	165.50
Lynda Schulman	1.90	140.00	266.00
Ellen Schaefer	7.50	125.00	937.50
TOTAL FEES DUE:			$2,908.50

PRIOR FEE APPLICATION

First Fee Application covering period of July 10, 1994 to January 25, 1995.

Fees Requested:	$18,398.00
Costs Requested:	589.26
Fees Authorized:	$10,000.00
Costs Authorized:	589.26

70

(D) SUMMARY OF TIME BY CATEGORY

CATEGORY	HOURS	PERCENT OF TOTAL
Administration	12.8	7.5
Amendments to Schedules	1.5	1
Communications with Trustee	.9	.5
Communications with Creditors	1.8	1
Court Appearances-Green v. Morgan Avenue Properties	1.8	1
Administration-Green v. Morgan Avenue Properties	.5	.3

PRIOR FEE APPLICATION July 10, 1994 through January 25, 1995

Administration	87.6	51.1
Preparation of Statements and Schedules	31.6	18.4
EL CORTEZ HOTEL TRANSACTION	9.1	5.3
Communications with Trustee	5.2	3.0
COMMUNICATIONS WITH CREDITORS	8.7	5.1
COMMUNICATIONS WITH COUNSEL FOR PROBATE ESTATE	6.1	3.6
COURT APPEARANCE AT 341(A) HEARING	1.2	.7
Administration-Green v. Morgan Avenue Properties	2.7	1.5
GRAND TOTAL:	171.5	100.0

At the first interim fee hearing held in this proceeding on June 3, 1995, the Court awarded a partial interim allowance of fees but requested counsel to defer from bringing a final fee application until the Trustee had had more time to administer this estate and determine if counsel's efforts assisted in minimizing the Trustee's efforts while maximizing the collections of assets. In March, 1996, the Trustee verbally advised counsel that it would now be appropriate to bring on for hearing the present final fee application.

III

FACTORS RELEVANT IN DETERMINING THE

ALLOWANCE OF FEES

The number of hours devoted to any one proceeding is only one factor in establishing a reasonable fee for legal services rendered. The reasonableness of the fee depends also on factors such as the complexity of the proceeding, the urgency of the problems and issues presented, the magnitude of the dollars involved and the results obtained. The time expended and the legal services performed on behalf of Morgan have been both reasonable and necessary. Applicant has and continues to work diligently to resolve the issues presented in this debtor's proceeding to the benefit of the estate and in a manner most economical to all concerned parties. The hourly rates used, computed and set forth hereinabove are a proper and equitable basis on which this Court may make allowance for fees.

The following attorneys, law clerks, and paralegals have

been involved in representing Morgan during the pendency of this case:

Flora L. Calem graduated from the University of Notre Dame Law School with a degree of Juris Doctor in May, 1977. She obtained her undergraduate degree at the University of California at San Diego. Ms. Calem has been a member of the Greenwich Bar since December 1977, and a member of the Bar for the United States Bankruptcy Court for the Southern District of Greenwich since December 1977. In addition, Mr. Calem served as a standing member of the panel of Trustees of the United States Bankruptcy Court, District of Greenwich, beginning on October 1, 1980 and completing her services on or about October of 1986.

During Flora L. Calem's career as an attorney and a Trustee of the United States Bankruptcy Court for the District of Greenwich, Ms. Calem has been involved in over 4000 bankruptcy cases ranging from the very largest to the very smallest.

Lauren S. Austin worked as a law clerk for Flora L. Calem, Inc. since October 1990, and became an associate of the firm in June 1992. Ms. Austin is a 1990 graduate of the Greenwich Western School of Law and is a member of the Greenwich Bar and the Bar of this District.

Holly Geulbaum is a 1990 graduate of the University of Bridgeport School of Law. She has been a member of the New York

State Bar since March 1991 and the Connecticut State Bar since September 1992. Ms. Geulbaum worked as a law clerk for Flora L. Calem from November 1993 until June 1994. She was an associate of the firm from June 1994 until July 1995. She has been employed as an associate for Calem & Austin since August 1, 1995. She has been a member of the Greenwich Bar and the Bar of this District since June 1994.

Ellen Schaefer is a 1988 graduate of the Greenwich Western School of Law. She is licensed with the Second Circuit Court of Appeals and the United States Supreme Court. She has been practicing exclusively in the area of insolvency counseling for almost four (4) years. She was been an associate with the firm of Calem & Austin from February of 1993 until July 31, 1995.

Lynda Schulman worked as a law clerk for Calem & Austin from November 1992. She subsequently became an associate of the firm in December 1992 and worked for the firm until July 31, 1995. Ms. Schulman is a 1992 graduate of Greenwich Western School of Law and is a member of the Greenwich Bar and the Bar of this District.

IV

COSTS ADVANCED

Attached hereto, marked as Exhibit "B" and incorporated herein by this reference as though set forth in full is a summary of   the costs advanced by applicant in representing Morgan on behalf of this estate from January 26, 1995 through and including March 29, 1996   in the amount of Two Hundred Sixty Two Dollars Eighty Three Cents ($262.83).

V

SOLE RECIPIENT

No agreement or understanding exists between applicant and any other person for the division or sharing of compensation for   services rendered or costs advanced in connection with this applicant's representation of Morgan.

VI

PRAYER

WHEREFORE, Applicant prays that following a hearing on this application, the court issue its order as follows:

1.   Approving the total attorney fees prayed for herein in the amount of $2908.50 and authorizing full payment thereon;

2.   Approving the total costs advanced prayed for herein in the amount of $262.83 and authorizing full payment thereon; and

3.   Confirming the prior award of fees and costs in the aggregate amount of Ten Thousand Five Hundred Eighty Nine Dollars and Twenty Six Cents ($10,589.26), and awarding payment of the

previously unapproved balance of Eight Thousand Three Hundred Ninety Eight Dollars ($8,398.00);

      4.   For such other and further relief as the court may deem just and proper.

                      Calem & HAYNES, A P.C.

Dated:_____   By:_____

                                      Flora L. Calem, Esq.
                                      Attorneys for Debtor,
                                      Morgan Avenue Properties

FORM 7.6

Notice to Creditors

United States Bankruptcy Court

	Case Number

_____ District of _____

NOTICE OF COMMENCEMENT OF CASE UNDER CHAPTER 7 OF THE BANKRUPTCY CODE.
MEETING OF CREDITORS, AND FIXING OF DATES
(Individual or Joint Debtor Asset Case)

In re (Name of Debtor)	Address of Debtor	Soc. Sec. / Tax Id. Nos.
	Date Case Filed (or Converted)	
Name and Address of Attorney for Debtor	Name and Address of Trustee	
Telephone Number		Telephone Number

☐ This is a converted case originally filed under chapter _____ on _____ (date).

FILING CLAIMS

Deadline to file a proof of claim:

DATE, TIME, AND LOCATION OF MEETING OF CREDITORS

DISCHARGE OF DEBTS

Deadline to File a Complaint Objecting to Discharge of the Debtor or to Determine Dischargeability of Certain Types of Debts:

COMMENCEMENT OF CASE. A petition for liquidation under chapter 7 of the Bankruptcy Code has been filed in this court by or against the person or persons named above as the debtor, and an order for relief has been entered. You will not receive notice of all documents filed in this case. All documents filed with the court, including lists of the debtor's property, debts, and property claimed as exempt are available for inspection at the office of the clerk of the bankruptcy court.

CREDITORS MAY NOT TAKE CERTAIN ACTIONS. A creditor is anyone to whom the debtor owes money or property. Under the Bankruptcy Code, the debtor is granted certain protection against creditors. Common examples of prohibited actions by creditors are contacting the debtor to demand repayment, taking action against the debtor to collect money owed to creditors or to take property of the debtor, and starting or continuing foreclosure actions, repossessions, or wage deductions. If unauthorized actions are taken by a creditor against a debtor, the court may penalize that creditor. A creditor who is considering taking action against the debtor or the property of the debtor should review § 362 of the Bankruptcy Code and may wish to seek legal advice. The staff of the clerk of the bankruptcy court is not permitted to give legal advice.

MEETING OF CREDITORS. The debtor (both husband and wife in a joint case) is required to appear at the meeting of creditors on the date and at the place set forth above for the purpose of being examined under oath. Attendance by creditors at the meeting is welcomed, but not required. At the meeting, the creditors may elect a trustee other than the one named above, elect a committee of creditors, examine the debtor, and transact such other business as may properly come before the meeting. The meeting may be continued or adjourned from time to time by notice at the meeting, without further written notice to creditors.

LIQUIDATION OF THE DEBTOR'S PROPERTY. The trustee will collect the debtor's property and turn any that is not exempt into money. If the trustee can collect enough money and property from the debtor, creditors may be paid some or all of the debts owed to them.

EXEMPT PROPERTY. Under state and federal law, the debtor is permitted to keep certain money or property as exempt. If a creditor believes that an exemption of money or property is not authorized by law, the creditor may file an objection. An objection must be filed not later than 30 days after the conclusion of the meeting of creditors.

DISCHARGE OF DEBTS. The debtor is seeking a discharge of debts. A discharge means that certain debts are made unenforceable against the debtor personally. Creditors whose claims against the debtor are discharged may never take action against the debtor to collect the discharged debts. If a creditor believes that the debtor should not receive any discharge of debts under § 727 of the Bankruptcy Code or that a debt owed to the creditor is not dischargeable under § 523(a)(2), (4), or (6) of the Bankruptcy Code, timely action must be taken in the bankruptcy court by the deadline set forth above in the box labeled "Discharge of Debts." Creditors considering taking such action may wish to seek legal advice.

PROOF OF CLAIM. Except as otherwise provided by law, in order to share in any payment from the estate, a creditor must file a proof of claim by the date set forth above in the box labeled "Filing Claims." The place to file the proof of claim, either in person or by mail, is the office of the clerk of the bankruptcy court. Proof of claim forms are available in the clerk's office of any bankruptcy court.

Address of the Clerk of the Bankruptcy Court	For the Court:
	Clerk of the Bankruptcy Court
	Date

Forms Inc. • P.O. Box 1109 • La Jolla, CA 92038 • 800/854-1080 • Official Form 9C

FORM 7.7

Notice of Hearing to Reaffirm a Debt

UNITED STATES BANKRUPTCY COURT
Southern District of California

In Re

Bankruptcy No.

_____
                Debtor.

NOTICE OF HEARING ON AGREEMENT TO REAFFIRM A DEBT

TO: CREDITOR:_____
                (Name and Address of Creditor)

      TRUSTEE:_____
                (Name and Address of Chapter 7 Trustee)

      UNITED STATES TRUSTEE:_____

      PLEASE TAKE NOTICE that the debtor in the above-entitled case has
calendared a hearing for approval of the accompanying Reaffirmation Agreement
pertaining to the debt of the creditor named above.

                HEARING DATE: _____

                HEARING TIME: _____

      The hearing will be held in DEPARTMENT NO. _____ of the United States
Bankruptcy Court, Fifth Floor, 940 Front Street, San Diego, California.

DATED:_____   _____
                                   (Signature of Debtor)
_____
                DECLARATION OF SERVICE BY MAIL

      I, the undersigned, declare under penalty of perjury that on _____
_____, 19___, I served a copy of the within Notice of Hearing for
Reaffirmation of a Debt, and a copy of the accompanying Reaffirmation
Agreement on the Creditor, the U.S. Trustee and Chapter 7 Trustee named above
by placing in the United States Mail a copy of the papers in separate
envelopes, each with postage fully prepaid and bearing the name and mailing
address of the addressee.

      Executed on _____, 19___, at _____, California.

                          _____
                                   Signature of Debtor)

FORM 7.8

Reaffirmation Agreement

B 240
(1/88)

REAFFIRMATION AGREEMENT

Debtor's Name	Bankruptcy Case No.

INSTRUCTIONS:

1) Write debtor's name and bankruptcy case number above.
2) Part A — Must be signed by both the debtor and the creditor.
3) Part B — Must be signed by the attorney who represents the debtor in this bankruptcy case.
4) Part C — Must be completed by the debtor if the debtor is not represented by an attorney in this bankruptcy case.
5) File the completed form by mailing or delivering to the Bankruptcy Clerk.
6) Attach written agreement, if any.

COURT USE ONLY

PART A — AGREEMENT

Creditor's Name and Address

Summary of Terms of the New Agreement

a) Principal Amount $ _____
   Interest Rate (APR) _____
   Monthly Payments $ _____
b) Description of Security: _____
   _____

Date Set for Discharge Hearing (If any)

Present Market Value $ _____

The parties understand that this agreement is purely voluntary and that the debtor may rescind the agreement at any time prior to discharge or within 60 days after such agreement is filed with the court, whichever occurs later, by giving notice of recission to the creditor.

_____
Date

_____
Signature of Debtor

_____
Signature of Creditor

_____
Signature of Joint Debtor

PART B — ATTORNEY'S DECLARATION

This agreement represents a fully informed and voluntary agreement that does not impose an undue hardship on the debtor or any dependent of the debtor.

_____
Date

_____
Signature of Debtor's Attorney

PART C — MOTION FOR COURT APPROVAL OF AGREEMENT — Complete only where debtor is not represented by an attorney.

I (we), the debtor, affirm the following to be true and correct:

1) I am not represented by an attorney in connection with this bankruptcy case.
2) My current monthly net income is $ _____
3) My current monthly expenses total $ _____, including any payment due under this agreement.
4) I believe that this agreement is in my best interest because _____
   _____
   _____

Therefore, I ask the court for an order approving this reaffirmation agreement.

_____
Date

_____
Signature of Debtor

_____
Signature of Joint Debtor

PART D — COURT ORDER

The court grants the debtor's motion and approves the voluntary agreement upon the terms specified above.

_____
Date

_____
Bankruptcy Judge

FORM 7.9

Discharge of Debtor

Form 18. DISCHARGE OF DEBTOR

[Caption as in Form 16A]

DISCHARGE OF DEBTOR

It appearing that a petition commencing a case under title 11, United States Code, was filed by or against the person named above on _____, and that an order for relief was entered under chapter 7, and that no complaint objecting to the discharge of the debtor was filed within the time fixed by the court [*or* that a complaint objecting to discharge of the debtor was filed and, after due notice and hearing, was not sustained];

IT IS ORDERED that

1. The above-named debtor is released from all dischargeable debts.

2. Any judgment heretofore or hereafter obtained in any court other than this court is null and void as a determination of the personal liability of the debtor with respect to any of the following:

    (a) debts dischargeable under 11 U.S.C. § 523;

    (b) unless heretofore or hereafter determined by order of this court to be nondischargeable, debts alleged to be excepted from discharge under clauses (2), (4) and (6) of 11 U.S.C. § 523(a);

    (c) debts determined by this court to be discharged.

3. All creditors whose debts are discharged by this order and all creditors whose judgments are declared null and void by paragraph 2 above are enjoined from instituting or continuing any action or employing any process or engaging in any act to collect such debts as personal liabilities of the above-named debtor.

Dated: _____

BY THE COURT

_____

United States Bankruptcy Judge.

COMMITTEE NOTE

This form previously was numbered Official Form No. 27. The form has been revised to accommodate cases commenced by the filing of either a voluntary or an involuntary petition.

FORM 8.1

Application to Convert a Chapter 7

Attorneys for Debtor-in-Possession

UNITED STATES BANKRUPTCY COURT
Southern District of California

In re	)	CASE NO. 95-7654-H11
	)	
HAPPY KIDS DAY CARE CENTER,	)	APPLICATION TO CONVERT CHAPTER 11 TO CHAPTER 7
	)	(11 U.S.C. § 1112(a))
	)	
	)	
	)	
	)	
Debtor-in-Possession.	)	

COMES NOW HAPPY KIDS DAY CARE CENTER, Debtor-in-Possession, by and through its counsel of record and makes application to the Court as follows:

1.   HAPPY KIDS DAY CARE CENTER has been acting as a debtor-in-possession pursuant to Chapter 11, Title 11 United States Code since September 17, 1995.

2.   HAPPY KIDS DAY CARE CENTER is qualified to be a debtor under Chapter 7 and desires that its Chapter 11 proceeding be converted to one under Chapter 7 of the Bankruptcy Code.

//

//

//

WHEREFORE, HAPPY KIDS DAY CARE CENTER prays that the Court enter its order converting its Chapter 11 proceeding to one under Chapter 7.

DATED:_____   By:_____
                                      Attorneys for Happy Kids Day Care
                                      Center, Inc.

FORM 8.2

Order Converting Case

B 221A
(1/88)

United States Bankruptcy Court

_____District of_____

In re

Bankruptcy Case No.

Debtor

ORDER CONVERTING CASE UNDER CHAPTER 11 TO CASE UNDER CHAPTER 7

☐ The debtor in possession has filed a motion in accordance with 11 U.S.C. § 1112(a), seeking to convert this case to a case under chapter 7 of the Bankruptcy Code (title 11 of the United States Code). The court finds that the case is not an involuntary case originally commenced under chapter 11, and that the case has not been converted to a case under chapter 11 on other than the debtor's request.

☐ A party in interest other than the debtor has filed a motion in accordance with 11 U.S.C. § 1112(b) seeking to convert the case to a case under chapter 7 of the Bankruptcy Code (title 11 of the United States Code). The court finds, after notice and a hearing, that the motion should be granted.

IT IS ORDERED THAT:

1. This chapter 11 case is converted to a case under chapter 7.
2. The debtor in possession or the chapter 11 trustee shall:
    a. forthwith turn over to the chapter 7 trustee all records and property of the estate under its custody and control as required by Bankruptcy Rule 1019(5); and
    b. within 30 days of the date of this order, file an accounting of all receipts and distributions made, together with a schedule of all unpaid debts incurred after the commencement of the chapter 11 case, as required by Bankruptcy Rule 1019(6).
3. The debtor within 15 days of the date of this order shall file the statements and schedules required by Bankruptcy Rules 1019(1)(A) & 1007(b), if such documents have not already been filed.
4. The debtor within 30 days of the date of this order shall if the case is converted after the confirmation of a plan, file:
    a. a schedule of all property not listed in the final report and account of the debtor in possession or chapter 11 trustee which was acquired after the commencement of the chapter 11 case but before the entry of this conversion order,
    b. a schedule of executory contracts entered into or assumed after the commencement of the chapter 11 case but before the entry of this conversion order, and
    c. a schedule of unpaid debts not listed in the final report and account of the debtor in possession or chapter 11 trustee which were incurred after the commencement of the chapter 11 case but before the entry of this conversion order, as required by Bankruptcy Rule 1019(6); and
    d. a statement of intention with respect to retention or surrender of property securing consumer debts, as required by 11 U.S.C. § 521(2)(A) and Bankruptcy Rule 1019(1)(B), and conforming to Official Form 8A.
5. [Other provisions as needed]

_____
Date

_____
Bankruptcy Judge

FORM 9.1

Objections to Debtor's Claim of Exemptions Combined
with Notice of Hearing

UNITED STATES BANKRUPTCY COURT
SOUTHERN DISTRICT OF CALIFORNIA
940 Front Street, Room 5-N-26, San Diego, California 92189-0020

In Re

BANKRUPTCY NO.

Debtor.

OBJECTIONS TO DEBTOR'S CLAIM OF EXEMPTIONS COMBINED WITH NOTICE OF HEARING

TO THE ABOVE-NAMED DEBTOR AND ATTORNEY OF RECORD, IF ANY:

    I, _____, hereby declare that I am:

    [ ] a creditor holding a claim against your estate,

    [ ] the trustee appointed to administer your estate,

and that I hereby object to your claim of exemption (Schedule B-4 or Schedule C) filed on

_____, 19_____, with specific reference to the following described

property of this estate:

    <u>Property Claimed Exempt</u>   <u>Reason for Objections</u>

    YOU ARE FURTHER NOTIFIED that hearing will be held in DEPARTMENT NO._____ of the

United States Bankruptcy Court located at 940 Front Street, Fifth Floor, San Diego,

California 92189-0020, on _____ at _____ .m.. at which time the

Court will consider and pass on these objections to your claims of exemptions.

DATED:

                                _____

                      [ ] Trustee   [ ] Creditor

CSD 1140

CSD 1140 (Page 2) [6/01/93]

CERTIFICATE OF SERVICE

I, the undersigned whose address appears below, certify:

That I am, and at all time hereinafter mentioned was, more than 18 years of age;

That on _____ day of _____, 19_____, I served a true copy of the within OBJECTIONS TO DEBTOR'S CLAIM OF EXEMPTIONS COMBINED WITH NOTICE OF HEARING by [describe here mode of service]:

on the following persons [set forth name and address of each person served] and as checked below:

[ ] For Chpt. 7, 11, & 12 cases:	[ ] For Chpt. 13 cases numbered 90-08445 or lower and ODD numbers beginning with 92-01217:	[ ] For Chpt. 13 cases numbered 90-08446 to 92-01215 and EVEN numbers beginning with 92-01216:
UNITED STATES TRUSTEE Department of Justice 101 West Broadway, Suite 440 San Diego, CA 92101	HARRY W. HEID, TRUSTEE Post Office Box 671 San Diego, CA 92112	DAVID L. SKELTON, TRUSTEE 620 "C" Street, Suite 413 San Diego, CA 92112-5312

I certify under penalty of perjury that the foregoing is true and correct.

Executed on _____
        (Date)

_____
(Typed Name and Signature)

_____
(Address)

_____
(City, State, ZIP Code)

CSD 1140

FORM 10.1

Representative United States Trustee Guidelines

U.S. Department of Justice

United States Trustee
Southern District of California

101 West Broadway, Suite 440
San Diego, California 92101

(619) 557-5013
FAX (619) 557-5339
FTS 895-5013
FAX 895-5339

GUIDELINES

FOR FULFILLING THE REQUIREMENTS

OF THE UNITED STATES TRUSTEE

GUIDELINES

FOR FULFILLING THE REQUIREMENTS
OF THE UNITED STATES TRUSTEE

TABLE OF CONTENTS		
Guideline No.	Title	Current Version Date
1	Service of Documents on United States Trustee	Oct. 20, 1989
2	Matters Requiring Submission to the United Trustee Prior to Filing with the Bankruptcy Court	Oct. 20, 1989
3	Applications to Authorize Employment of Professional Persons	Oct. 20, 1989
4	Applications for Allowance of Compensation and Expenses for Professional Persons	Jan. 15, 1989
5	Disclosure Statements	Jan. 15, 1989
6	Chapter 11 Quarterly Fee Payments	Oct. 20, 1989

In addition to the Guidelines, the United States Trustee has promulgated Operating And Reporting Requirements For Chapter 11 Debtors-In-Possession pursuant to 28 U.S.C. 586(a)(3) and Bankruptcy Local Rule 2015-1. Copies are available in the Office of United States Trustee, Suite 440, 101 West Broadway, San Diego, California, 92101.

OFFICE OF THE UNITED STATES TRUSTEE

GUIDELINE NO. 1

SERVICE OF DOCUMENTS ON UNITED STATES TRUSTEE

A. **SERVICE OF DOCUMENTS**

The following documents shall be served upon the Office of the United States Trustee:

1. **Cases**

    (a) Any document filed in cases under Chapters 7, 11 and 12 of the Bankruptcy Code, except proofs of claims, and except petitions and accompanying materials that are included in the initial filing with the Bankruptcy Court.

2. **Adversary Proceedings**

    (a) Any document filed in any adversary proceeding related to a case under Chapter 11 if such document is required to be filed with the Bankruptcy Court.

    (b) Any document filed in any adversary proceeding where a Bankruptcy Trustee is named as a party defendant.

    (c) Complaints objecting to the debtors' discharge under Section 727.

B. **MANNER OF SERVICE**

All such documents which are filed with the Bankruptcy Court and which must be served in accordance with this rule shall be accompanied by proof of service on the Office of the United States Trustee, Suite 440, 101 West Broadway, San Diego, California, 92101.

C. **REFERENCE**

See Bankruptcy Rules 2002, X-1008, X-1009(b).

(10/20/89)

OFFICE OF THE UNITED STATES TRUSTEE

GUIDELINE NO. 2

MATTERS REQUIRING SUBMISSION TO THE UNITED STATES TRUSTEE
PRIOR TO FILING WITH THE BANKRUPTCY COURT

Prior to filing any of the following motions or applications in the bankruptcy court, a moving party shall first obtain a Statement of Position of the United States Trustee with respect to the motion or application in accordance with Bankruptcy Local Rules (BLR) 9013-5(c)(2), 1007-4, 2014-1, 6005-2, and 4002-2:

A.   Motions for Extension of Time for filing schedules and statements required by BLR 1007;

B.   Applications to Employ attorneys or other professionals by a Debtor-in-Possession or trustee pursuant to BLR 2014-1 and 6005;*

C.   Applications for Entry of Final Decree on consummation of a Chapter 11 plan pursuant to Bankruptcy Rule (BR) 2015;

D.   Motions for interim compensation to a Debtor or insider pursuant to BLR 4002-2(b).

To obtain the Statement of Position of the United States Trustee, the moving party shall serve a copy of the motion or application, the proposed order, and a proof of service (hereinafter "the motion papers"), together with a self-addressed envelope on the United States Trustee.

The United States Trustee will review the motion papers and serve upon the moving party a Statement of Position of the United States Trustee with respect to the motion or application, no later than five (5) business days from the date of service, if personally served, and eight (8) business days from the date of service, if served by mail.

Thereafter, the moving party may proceed to file with the court the motion papers together with the Statement of Position of the United States Trustee.

---

*See also Guideline No. 3, infra, Applications to Employ Professional Persons.

(10/20/89)

110

GUIDELINE NO. 3

APPLICATIONS TO AUTHORIZE EMPLOYMENT OF PROFESSIONAL PERSONS

An application to authorize employment of a professional person must, at a minimum, comply with BANKRUPTCY RULE 2014(a) and the following requirements:

1. It must be signed by a person authorized to make the Application such as the Debtor-in-Possession, the Chapter 11 Trustee, or an officer, general partner or other principal of the Debtor-in-Possession.

2. It must state facts showing the necessity for such employment.

3. It must state the name of the person(s) or the firm to be employed.

4. It must state the reason for the selection of the particular professional to be employed. (Attachment of a statement of the past experience of the professional should be included.)

5. It must state the specific services to be rendered in connection with the employment.

6. It must state whether the person to be employed is a disinterested person or holds or represents an interest adverse to the debtor or the estate. It must be accompanied by a verified statement of the person to be employed setting forth the person's connections, if any, with the debtor, creditors, any other party in interest, or their respective attorneys and accountants. The verified statement should not merely state legal conclusions, but it should set forth facts disclosing connections with the parties, past or present. It should also state whether the professional person rendered services within one year prior to the filing of the instant petition, the value of those services, when such services were paid and the source of such payment, to the best of his or her knowledge.

7. It must state the amount and source of any retainer previously received and the terms and conditions of employment, including the then current hourly rate(s) charged by each type of professional expected to render services, including partners, associates, and paraprofessional persons employed by the professional whose services will be utilized for the benefit of and whose time will be charged to the Estate. No retainer may be paid to counsel post-petition in the absence of a Court Order authorizing the payment.

(10/20/89)

111

8. It must include a statement that no compensation will be paid by the Debtor-in-Possession or any other person or entity for services rendered to the estate, or by the Chapter 11 Trustee except upon application and entry of an Order by the Court authorizing payment. [See In re Knudsen, 84 B.R. 668 (9th Cir. BAP 1988)].

9. It must include a copy of the proposed Order approving the employment.

10. If an application to employ a professional by the Debtor-in-Possession or Chapter 11 Trustee is made more than thirty (30) days after the date of commencement of post-petition services by that professional, an explanation of the delay in the form of an affidavit must accompany the application. Any application seeking an Order nunc pro tunc more than 30 days should be noticed to all creditors and state the amount of fees and expenses which have accrued during the period between the date of the commencement of post-petition services and the date of the Application to Authorize Employment.

11. If more than one counsel is being retained to represent the Debtor-in-Possession, the Chapter 11 Trustee or the Creditors' Committee, there should be facts stated in the application as to the need for dual counsel, the services to be preformed by each, and an affirmative statement in each application that there will be no duplication of services.

SPECIAL NOTES:

1. Refer to Attorney Practice Guideline No. 4 (Applications for Payment of Professional Fees) for further details as to items in Fee/Expense Applications which are considered appropriate and inappropriate by the United States Trustee.

2. When the Debtor-in-Possession or Trustee has been authorized to employ a professional person, any successor professional must obtain similar court authorization for such employment pursuant to section 327 of the BANKRUPTCY CODE and BANKRUPTCY RULE 2014. The Application to Authorize Employment must be submitted and approved prior to the successor professional commencing services on behalf of the Debtor-in-Possession or Chapter 11 Trustee. When there is a change in attorneys, the filing of a Substitution of Attorney form is also required.

3. For applications that seek nunc pro tunc approval, counsel are referred to In re THC Financial Corp., 837 F.2d. 389 (9th Cir. 1988), In re Crook, 79 B.R. 475 (9th Cir. BAP 1987); In re Mahoney Trocki Associates, 54 B.R. 823 (Bkcy, S.D. Cal. 1985); In re Kroeger Properties and Development Inc., 57 B.R. 821 (9th Cir. BAP 1986).

(10/20/89)

OFFICE OF THE UNITED STATES TRUSTEE

GUIDELINE NO. 4

APPLICATIONS FOR ALLOWANCE OF COMPENSATION
AND EXPENSES FOR PROFESSIONAL PERSONS

Applications for allowance of compensation and expenses for professional persons should conform with Bankruptcy Rule 2016 and the following substantive requirements:

1. The application should recite the date of entry of the Order of the Bankruptcy Court approving the employment of the individual or firm for whom payment of fees and/or expenses is sought, the date of the last Fee Application for that professional, and the amount of fees and expenses previously requested, approved by the Court and received.

2. The application should contain first a summary breakdown of the services provided including dates, type of service, results, and the total time per professional, attributable to the service. Examples of types of services include, but are not limited to: relief from stay, cash collateral; disclosure statement; plan; fee application; adversary proceeding; transactional matters and miscellaneous services.

3. The application should include a detailed listing of all time spent by the professional on matters for which compensation is sought.

    A. Date service was rendered.

    B. Description of service--(It is not sufficient to merely state "Research", "Telephone Call:, "Court Appearance", etc. Reference must be made to the particular persons, motions, discrete tasks performed and other matters related to such service. Summaries that list a number of services under only one time period will not be satisfactory.)

    C. Amount of time spent--(Summaries are not adequate. Time spent is to be broken down in detail by the specific task performed. Lumping services together is not satisfactory.)

    D. Designation of the particular person who rendered the service--(If more than one person's services are included in the application, specify which person performed each service.)

(1/15/89)

113

4. An application that seeks reimbursement of expenses should include a summary listing of all expenses by category (i.e. long distance telephone, travel deposition, witness fees and filing fees). As to unusual or costly expense items, as to each such item, the application must state:

   A. Date the expense was incurred.

   B. Description of the expense.

   C. Amount of the expense.

   D. Explanation of the need for the expense.

5. The application should contain a listing of the hourly rates charged by each person whose services form a basis for the fees requested. A summary in substantially the following form should be included in the application:

Attorney Name	Hourly Rate	Total Hours this application	Total Fee Due

6. The following items are considered inappropriate for Fee and/or Expense Applications. Any application containing such items may be objected to by the United States Trustee:

   A. Minimum hourly billing increments of greater than 0.10 hours.

   B. Compensation sought for services rendered prior to the effective date of the Order approving employment of the professional. (This does not apply to the pre-petition services rendered by Bankruptcy counsel in preparing the case for filing or services rendered during the maximum thirty (30) day delay between the filing of the petition and the filing of the application to employ debtor's general bankruptcy counsel).

   C. Compensation sought from the estate for services rendered prior to the date of the filing of the Petition except for bankruptcy-related services.

   D. Requests for compensation for services performed by an attorney employed by a trustee for matters properly within the responsibility of the trustee.

(1/15/89)

114

E.   An attorney/trustee failing to segregate
     properly those services performed as an
     "attorney" versus those performed in the
     capacity of "trustee".

F.   Requests for compensation for services rendered
     which were unnecessary, unreasonable, or in
     error.

G.   Requests for reimbursement of customary
     overhead expenses such as secretarial and word
     processing costs, without a showing of just
     cause. (Reimbursement of reasonable Westlaw and
     Lexis cost is acceptable.)

H.   Requests for reimbursement of expenses not yet
     incurred or compensation for work not yet
     performed as of the date of the hearing.

I.   Photocopy charges in excess of the actual cost
     or twenty (.20) cents per page, whichever is
     less, without a showing of good cause.

J.   Excessive long distance telephone calls which
     are not justified.

K.   Extraordinary mailing expenses which are not
     justified, e.g., excessive use of Express Mail.

L.   Failure to give adequate written notice of the
     Fee and/or Expense Application.

M.   Filing of a Fee and/or Expense Application more
     frequently than once every 120 days without a
     prior Bankruptcy Court Order allowing more
     frequent applications.

N.   Requests for compensation at the full rate of
     the professional for performing non-
     professional services such as document delivery
     or filing of pleadings.

O.   Submitting Fee Applications for a Debtor-in-
     Possession; or Trustee's Professionals at a
     time when the Debtor-in-Possession or Chapter
     11 Trustee have failed to pay Quarterly Fees or
     have failed to file timely Operating Reports or
     Interim Statements.

7.   Special Note regarding Required Final Fee Applications:
     Within a reasonable time after confirmation of a plan of
     reorganization, all professionals who have been
     employed by the Debtor or Trustee are required to file
     a Final Fee Application. The Final Fee Application is

                                                  (1/15/89)

                          115

to cover all of the services performed in the case and must seek approval of all prior interim fee awards. The Application may not merely cover the last period for which fees are sought.

8. References: Applications for payment of professional fees and expenses, see generally Bankruptcy Code Sections 328, 329, 330 and 331. See also, In re Manoa Finance Company, 853 F.2d 687 (9th Cir. 1988); Clark v. Los Angeles, 803 F.2d 987 (9th Cir.); In re Yermakov, 718 F.2d. 1465 (9th Cir. 1983); In re Knudsen, 84 B.R. 668 (9th Cir. BAP 1988); In re Confections by Sandra, Inc., 83 B.R. 729 (9th Cir. BAP 1987); In re Wavelength, 61 B.R. 614 (9th Cir. BAP 1986); In re Powerline Oil Co., 71 B.R. 767 (9th Cir. BAP 1986) In re Weingarden, 84 B.R. 691 (Bkcy. S.D. Cal. 1988); In re Riverside-Linden Investment Co., 85 B.R. 107 (Bkcy. S.D. Cal. 1988). In re Wildman, 72 B.R. 700 (Bkcy. N.D. Ill. 1987).

(1/15/89)

OFFICE OF THE UNITED STATES TRUSTEE

GUIDELINE NO. 5

DISCLOSURE STATEMENTS

Disclosure Statements are required to contain adequate information in accordance with 11 U.S.C. 1125. The following is a checklist of items that should generally appear in Disclosure Statements. The list is neither exclusive nor exhaustive and, depending upon the size and nature of the Debtor and the Plan, may vary considerably.

1. **Purpose of the Disclosure Statement:** The Disclosure Statement should indicate that its purpose is to provide "adequate information" of a kind, and in sufficient detail, as far as is reasonably practicable in light of the nature and history of the debtor and the condition of the debtor's books and records, that would enable a hypothetical, reasonable investor typical of holders of claims (creditors) or interests (shareholders) of the relevant class to make an informed judgement concerning the Plan. [See 11 U.S.C. 1125(a)].

2. **Vote Required for Approval:** The Disclosure Statement should briefly indicate the vote required for approval of the Plan and should clearly indicate that the creditors or interest holders have a choice: they can either vote for or against the Plan. It should also state that creditors have accepted the Plan if voting creditors holding at least two-thirds in amount and more than one-half in number of the allowed claims voting, have voted for the Plan. [See 11 U.S.C. 1126(c)].

3. **Description of the Plan:** The Disclosure Statement should give a description of the major provisions of the Plan, including, where feasible, an estimated date by which creditors could expect to receive payment, an expected percentage return on their claims, and a summary of the treatment of various classes under the Plan. Generally the description does not have to be detailed and may merely refer to the Plan which contains such detailed information. Further, the summary should contain a description of each class of creditors and the approximate dollar amount of the claims in each class.

4. **Means of effectuating the Plan:** The Disclosure Statement should indicate how the debtor intends to accomplish the goals of the Plan, _i.e._, whether by infusion of cash by an investor, sale of real property, continued business operation, issuance of stock or otherwise. If an investor is to provide funds, financial information regarding the investor's ability to provide such funds should be included.

(1/15/89)

117

5. **Cash Requirements:** The Disclosure Statement should indicate the amount of cash to be paid upon confirmation of the Plan to satisfy administrative claims and any other claims and the source of such cash. If the debtor expects a cash infusion from an outside source or from principals which is to be repaid in the future, then the identity of the source as well as the repayment terms should be disclosed. Similarly, the effect of such repayment (i.e., principal and interest payments) should be reflected in the projections.

6. **Administrative Expenses:** The Disclosure Statement should indicate whether any administrative expenses have accrued which must be paid at the time of confirmation, unless the party to whom the expenses are owed has consented to an alternative treatment. [See 11 U.S.C. 1129(a)(9)(A)]. Such disclosure should include the expected amounts owed, the identity of the claimants, and the source of the funds from which they will be paid upon confirmation.

7. **Legal Proceedings:** The Disclosure Statement should briefly describe all material legal proceedings to which the debtor is a party, proceedings. which the debtor contemplates instituting, and legal proceedings which are known to be threatened against the Debtor. The information should include the court in which the litigation is pending, its present status, the relief sought, the debtor's prognosis for the outcome, the estimated litigation costs and the effect, if any, on the Plan.

8. **Description of the Business:** The Disclosure Statement should describe the debtor's business, including those factors which may be unusual or peculiar to the business, such as seasonal cycles and unique product lines.

9. **Reasons for Financial Difficulties and Corrections of those Factors:** The Disclosure Statement should contain a brief narrative description of the reasons for the debtor's financial difficulties and the steps taken to alleviate the situation since the inception of the case.

10. **Valuation of Assets:** In conjunction with any projections or any liquidation analysis, the Disclosure Statement should contain a current Balance Sheet and Profit and Loss Statement. The Balance Sheet should indicate whether or not such Statement was audited and the basis for the valuation of indicated items. Further, the Disclosure Statement should indicate, possibly in a separate schedule, the current values of assets and the source of such estimated values (i.e., cost or appraisals).

(1/15/89)

11. **Historical and Current Financial Information:** The Disclosure Statement should include historical and current financial data, including Profit and Loss and Cash Flow Statements, and Balance Sheets to give creditors some perspective on both the debtor's past and current financial situation and its prospects under the Plan. A pro forma Balance Sheet as of the date that the plan will be confirmed indicating the financial condition of the reorganized debtor should be included. In order to allow a full analysis, Profit and Loss Statements must be provided on both a cash and accrual basis.

12. **Liquidation Analysis:** A creditor cannot make an informed judgement regarding a Plan without information as to available alternatives. Consequently, there should be some analysis as to what creditors would receive in a Chapter 7 liquidation. The Disclosure Statement should clearly indicate the difference between treatment accorded in the he Plan and that which creditors would receive under a Chapter 7 liquidation. Such a comparison might indicate the percentage return to creditors under each alternative and might include assumptions regarding liquidation values, administrative costs, etc. A disclosure of any assumption utilized by management in formulating a liquidation alternative should be disclosed. [See 11 U.S.C. 1129(a)(7)(ii)]. It is generally insufficient to merely indicate that the Plan will provide a better return than liquidation without any supporting information. A simple tabular presentation setting forth estimated administrative expenses, priority expenses, secured and unsecured claims, together with the debtor's estimated asset values (including sources of such values) is appropriate. The liquidation analysis should also provide a present value calculation of the payments to creditors under the proposed Plan versus its respective class liquidation amount.

13. **Projections:** Projections are critical to a creditor's ability to assess the viability of the Plan, especially where the Plan calls for deferred payments to creditors and is based upon future earnings. The Statement should include projections as far into the future as is practicable, including assumptions used by the debtor in formulating the projections, such as expected sales levels, gross and net profit levels, and inventory acquisition. At a minimum, the period covered by the projections should be commensurate with the period of payment deferral under the Plan. Use of spreadsheets is encouraged. Financial projections must be provided on both a cash and accrual basis.

(1/15/89)

14. **Marketing Efforts:** The Disclosure Statement should indicate what efforts the debtor has made since the filing to market its properties that are currently for sale. Such a description should include the identity of the listing agent, the listing price, any offers received or anticipated, pending litigation which might affect the sale of the property, the equity in the property (including the source of the valuation), and any alternatives for marketing the property in the future.

15. **Post-Petition Events:** The Disclosure Statement should indicate whether any major post-petition events have occurred which might affect the case, such as the appointment of a Creditors' Committee, a trustee, an examiner or the existence of litigation with significant consequences to the ability of the debtor to meet the Plan requirements.

16. **Management Compensation:** The Disclosure Statement should disclose the identities of top management, a description of their qualification, and their salary levels. [See 11 U.S.C. 1129(a)(5)]. Further, any disclosure should include the identity and affiliations of any individual proposed to serve, after confirmation of the Plan, as director, officer or voting trustee of the debtor, an affiliate of the debtor participating in a joint Plan with the debtor, or a successor to the debtor under the Plan, and the identity of any insider who will be employed or retained by the reorganized debtor and the nature of any compensation for such insider.

17. **Insider and Affiliate Claims:** The Disclosure Statement should disclose the claims asserted by insiders as defined by 11 U.S.C. 101(30). This disclosure should include the identity of the claimant, the affiliation of the insider with the debtor, the circumstances giving rise to the claim and the amount of the claim, the amount the insider is asserting as a creditor and/or whether any or all his claims have been subordinated.

18. **Stock Issued for Debt:** If the debtor plans to issue stock for all or part of its debt, the Disclosure Statement should indicate if such stock is exempt from securities laws under 11 U.S.C. 1145 and should describe the nature of the stock or securities, such as voting rights, interest rate, cumulation of dividends, liquidation preference, potential markets and market values after confirmation, and the existence of other classes of stock. The debtor should state stock is registered under section 5 of the S.E.C. Act or, if not, what exemption from registration is claimed and the basis for such a claim.

(1/15/89)

120

Further, if the exemption of 11 U.S.C. 1145 is relied
upon, the the Disclosure Statement should indicate
that the following legend, with appropriate changes,
will be included on any issued securities:

"The securities represented by this certificate
 have not been registered under the Securities Act
 of 1933 and were issued pursuant to an exemption
 provided by 11 U.S.C. 1145, under an order confirming
 Plan in a case entitled_____, Debtor
 Case No._____ in the United States Bankruptcy
 Court for the Southern District of California. The
 holder of this certificate is referred to 11 U.S.C.
 1145(b) and (c) for guidance as to the sale of these
 securities."

19. U.S. Trustee Quarterly Fees: The Plan should state that
     any unpaid quarterly fees will be paid in full prior to
     or on the effective date of the Plan. In this regard,
     Bankruptcy Code, Section 1129(a)(12) provides that a
     plan may not be confirmed unless all fees payable by
     Debtor under 28 U.S.C. 1930 have been paid or the plan
     provides for the payment of all such fees on the
     effective date of the plan.

(1/15/89)

121

OFFICE OF THE UNITED STATES TRUSTEE

GUIDELINE NO. 6

CHAPTER 11 QUARTERLY FEE PAYMENTS

Pursuant to the BANKRUPTCY JUDGES, UNITED STATES TRUSTEE, AND FAMILY FARMER BANKRUPTCY ACT of 1986, all Debtors-In-Possession and Trustees in Chapter 11 cases pending in the Southern District of California are required to pay quarterly fees to the United States Trustee. These quarterly fee requirements are specified in Section 1930(a)(6) of Title 28 of the United States Code.

The fee must be paid to the United States Trustee every calendar quarter from the time the Petition is filed*, until the date an Order is entered confirming plan, or dismissing or converting the case. Quarterly fees must be paid on or before the effective date of a plan of reorganization in order to be confirmed by the Court. [11 U.S.C. Section 1129 (a)(12)]. FAILURE TO PAY THE QUARTERLY FEE IS CAUSE FOR CONVERSION OR DISMISSAL OF THE CHAPTER 11 CASE. [Section 1112(b)(10) of the BANKRUPTCY CODE].

The amount of the fee will depend on the amount of disbursements made from the estate assets. A minimum fee of $250 is due each quarter for every pending Chapter 11 case. Fees are owed even if no disbursements are made during the quarter, and even if the Debtor does not operate business. Also, a Chapter 11 case pending even one day during the quarter requires payment of the fee for that period.

Fee payment is due no later than one (1) month following the quarterly reporting period, calculated according to the following schedule:

FEE SCHEDULE

TOTAL QUARTERLY DISBURSEMENTS			QUARTERLY FEE
No Disbursements			$ 250
$ 0	to	$ 14,999.99	$ 250
$ 15,000	to	$ 149,999.99	$ 500
$ 150,000	to	$ 299,999.99	$ 1,250
$ 300,000	to	$ 2,999,999.99	$ 3,750
$ 3,000,000	to	and above	$ 5,000

    * Cases filed prior to November 26, 1986, and which are currently pending under Chapter 11 are assessed with quarterly fee payments beginning October 20, 1989. [Public Law 99-554, 100, Stat. 388, Section 302 (e)(2) (1986)].

Requests for voluntary dismissals will be objected to unless all fees have been paid in full. If a Debtor-in-Possession or Chapter 11 Trustee has failed to provide reports that substantiate disbursements during the applicable quarter, the United States Trustee may require payment of the maximum fee for each unpaid quarter.

Quarterly fees are to be made payable to THE UNITED STATES TRUSTEES and are to be mailed to the address in Georgia set forth below. Only fees and billing statements are to be mailed. No further documentation will be accepted at this address. Fees are not to be mailed or delivered to the local Office of the United States Trustee unless otherwise specified. If any check is returned "unpaid" for any reason, all subsequent payments must be made by way of cashier's check, certified check or money order. It is recommended that upon confirmation of a plan, the last quarterly fee, together with any delinquent fees, be paid by way of cashier's check, certified check, or money order.

To ensure proper credit, it is imperative that Debtors-in-Possession and Chapter 11 Trustees write the case Account Number on each check and return it with the Payment Coupon provided with the quarterly billings. A separate check and coupon should be sent for each quarterly payment even if more than one quarterly fee is paid at the same time.

Payments should be mailed to the following address unless otherwise directed by the United States Trustee's office:

UNITED STATES TRUSTEES
P.O. BOX 198246
Atlanta, GA 30384

(10/20/89)

UNITED STATES TRUSTEE
SOUTHERN DISTRICT OF CALIFORNIA
GUIDELINE FOR REVIEW OF CHAPTER 13 ATTORNEY FEES

The United States Trustee, pursuant to her duties to supervise the administration of Chapter 13 cases, will monitor Disclosures of Compensation Paid and Applications for Compensation, and will reserve the right in every case to require strict compliance with Rule 2016 of the Bankruptcy Rules. The United States Trustee generally will not require detailed application in Chapter 13 cases where the compensation paid, or to be paid, does not exceed:

a.1. $995.00   **for the fees and expenses, other than filing fees, for services rendered or to be rendered in Chapter 13 consumer cases prior to the confirmation, dismissal, or conversion, whichever first occurs.**

a.2. $1,295.00   **for the fees and expenses, other than filing fees, for services rendered or to be rendered in Chapter 13 business cases prior to the confirmation, dismissal, or conversion, whichever first occurs. This amount takes into consideration the additional time required to prepare the Engaged in Business Statement of Affairs, an itemized list of all business assets, and a profit and loss statement, by month for at least three months prior to the filing.**

b. $330.00   **for the fee and expenses for services rendered post-confirmation for the preparation, filing, noticing and hearings in regard to a debtor's modified plan under Section 1329 of the Bankruptcy Code.**

c. $250.00   **for the fee and expenses of all services rendered in opposition to Motions to Modify or Vacate Automatic Stay.**

d. $250.00   **for the fee and expenses of all services rendered for obtaining an Order authorizing the sale or refinancing of real estate, whether the order is obtained by stipulation or after noticed hearing.**

e. $150.00   **for the fee and expenses of all services rendered for the preparation, filing,**

noticing, and hearings in regard to
objections to a claim.

f. $150.00   for the fee and expenses of all services
                  rendered for the preparation, filing,
                  noticing, and hearings in opposition to
                  a petition to dismiss the case.

g. $ 75.00   for each continuance of a post-
                  confirmation hearing, not including
                  debtor's Modified Plan hearings.

These amounts are not to be considered as recommendations by
the United States Trustee as to the reasonableness of an attorney
fee in a given case. In the event fee and expense requests are
cumulatively greater than the guideline amounts, the United
States Trustee will require strict compliance with Rule 2016 of
the Bankruptcy Rules, whereby an application is filed showing the
services rendered, time expended, and expenses incurred for a
period one year before the filing of the petition commencing the
case to the date of the application for fees.

Effective Date: For each case
in which First Meeting of
Creditors is held on or after
June 1, 1991

FORM 12.1

Notice of Filing a Motion for Relief from Automatic Stay

CSD 1185 [6/01/93]
Name, Address, Telephone No. & I.D. No.

UNITED STATES BANKRUPTCY COURT
SOUTHERN DISTRICT OF CALIFORNIA
940 Front Street, Room 5-N-26, San Diego, California 92189-0020

In Re	
Debtor.	**BANKRUPTCY NO.**
Moving Party	**RS NO.**
Respondent(s)	

NOTICE OF FILING OF A MOTION FOR RELIEF FROM AUTOMATIC STAY

TO THE ABOVE NAMED RESPONDENT(S)[1]:

YOU ARE HEREBY NOTIFIED that a Motion for Relief from the Automatic Stay provided by §362 of the Bankruptcy Code has been filed. If you object to the Court granting relief from the automatic stay as requested in the Motion, **YOU MUST, WITHIN 11[2] DAYS FOLLOWING THE DATE OF SERVICE OF THIS NOTICE OF MOTION ON YOU:**

1. Obtain a hearing date and time from the appropriate Courtroom Deputy for the judge assigned to this bankruptcy case. *If a Chapter 7, 11, or 12 case*, determine which deputy to call by looking at the Bankruptcy Case No. in the above caption of this notice. If the case number contains the letter(s):

-	M	-	call (619) 557-6019	-	DEPARTMENT ONE
-	A	-	call (619) 557-6594	-	DEPARTMENT TWO
-	H	-	call (619) 557-6018	-	DEPARTMENT THREE
-	B	-	call (619) 557-5157	-	DEPARTMENT FOUR

    For ALL Chapter 13 cases, call (619) 557-5955.

2. File with the undersigned Clerk of the Bankruptcy Court, at the address shown above, the original and one copy of:
    (a) a "DECLARATION IN OPPOSITION TO THE MOTION"[2]; and
    (b) a separate "REQUEST AND NOTICE OF HEARING ON MOTION," using Form CSD 1186 of this Court (this form must be obtained from the Office of the undersigned Clerk);

3. Serve a copy of both documents on the [Attorney for the] Moving Party named in the upper left hand corner.

4. Serve a copy of both documents on each of the additional parties as required by Bankruptcy Local Rule 4001-3.

    IF YOU FAIL TO FILE WITH THE CLERK AND SERVE ON THE MOVING PARTY YOUR REQUEST FOR HEARING AND THE DECLARATION IN OPPOSITION TO MOTION WITHIN THE 11-DAY[2] PERIOD PROVIDED BY THIS MOTION, THE COURT MAY GRANT THE MOVING PARTY RELIEF FROM THE AUTOMATIC STAY WITHOUT FURTHER NOTICE TO YOU OR A HEARING.

Dated: Barry K. Lander, Clerk

                                By:_____, Deputy Clerk

ALL PLEADINGS RELATED TO THIS PARTICULAR RS ACTION MUST CONTAIN THE ABOVE CAPTION

[1] Bankruptcy Local Rule 4001-2, printed on the reverse side, governs service of this notice.
[2] If you were served by mail, you have three (3) additional days to take the above-stated actions. Instructions for the Respondent and the date of service of this notice indicated in the Certificate of Service are printed on the reverse side.

CSD 1185   (RECEIPT NO._____)   [Continued on Page 2]

CSD 1185 (Page 2) [5/01/93]

1. **ALL PLEADINGS RELATED TO THIS PARTICULAR RS ACTION MUST CONTAIN THE ABOVE CAPTION.**
2. **INSTRUCTIONS TO RESPONDENT:** If you file a "Declaration in Opposition to the Motion," it must be signed by the respondent under oath; and
   (1) identify the interest of the Respondent in the property;
   (2) state with particularity the grounds for the opposition; and
   (3) if respondent is the debtor or the trustee, state the provable value of the property specified in the Motion and the amount of equity which would be realized by the debtor after deduction of all encumbrances.
3. **INSTRUCTIONS TO MOVING PARTY:** Bankruptcy Local Rule 4001-2 provides that: "(a) A motion for stay relief shall:
   "(1) name, as respondents, the debtor, the trustee, and other entities entitled to receive notice of default or notice of sale under applicable non-bankruptcy law governing foreclosure of real or personal property which is the subject of the motion, or the agents for such parties;
   "(2) state with particularity the relief or order sought, and the grounds for such relief or order;
   "(3) state the status of any pending foreclosure or repossession;
   "(4) if the basis of the motion is lack of equity or adequate protection, and value is relevant, state by declaration the provable value of the subject property and the amount of any known encumbrances. The declaration shall also contain a statement as to the competency of the declarant and the foundation for any opinion therein; and
   "(5) if the motion is brought for cause, state by declaration or other verified pleading the specific facts that constitute such cause.
      "(b) Failure to set forth the information required by this rule may be grounds for denial of the relief requested.
      "(c) The moving party shall serve the motion, together with Local Form CSD 1185 (Note: new form number), NOTICE OF FILING OF A MOTION FOR RELIEF FROM AUTOMATIC STAY, as set forth in Appendix C, on the parties named in Bankruptcy Local Rule 4001-2(a)(1) above. In a chapter 11 or 12 case, a copy of the motion shall also be served on the United States Trustee.
      "(d) The proof of service shall be filed with the clerk no later than the next business day following the date of service."

** MOTIONS FILED <u>AFTER</u> THE CASE IS CLOSED ARE NOT ENTITLED TO A REFUND OF FEES **
= =
[The below Certification of Service must accompany the Notice of Motion printed on the reverse and any motion for entry of a default order pursuant to Bankruptcy Local Rule 4001-6.]

CERTIFICATE OF SERVICE

I, the undersigned whose address appears below, certify:

That I am, and at all times hereinafter mentioned was, more than 18 years of age;

That on _____ [DATE OF SERVICE[3]], I served a true copy of the within NOTICE OF FILING OF A MOTION FOR RELIEF FROM AUTOMATIC STAY, together with a copy of the Motion for Relief from Stay and [describe any other papers]:

by [describe mode of service]:

on the following persons [set forth name and address of each person served] and as checked below:

[ ] For Chpt. 11 & 12 cases:	[ ] For Chpt. 13 cases numbered 90-08445 or lower and ODD numbers beginning with 92-01217:	[ ] For Chpt. 13 cases numbered 90-08446 to 92-01215 and EVEN numbers beginning with 92-01216:
UNITED STATES TRUSTEE Department of Justice 101 West Broadway, Suite 440 San Diego, CA 92101	HARRY W. HEID, TRUSTEE Post Office Box 671 San Diego, CA 92112	DAVID L. SKELTON, TRUSTEE 620 "C" Street, Suite 413 San Diego, CA 92112-5312

I certify under penalty of perjury that the foregoing is true and correct.

Executed on _____
(Date)

_____
(Typed Name and Signature)

_____
(Address)

_____
(City, State, ZIP Code)

[3]This DATE OF SERVICE commences the time period for responding to Motion.
CSD 1185

FORM 12.2

Motion for Relief from Automatic Stay

Attorneys for Debtor

UNITED STATES BANKRUPTCY COURT
Southern District of California

In re	) CASE NO.95-7654-H11
	)
HAPPY KIDS DAY CAR CENTER,	) MOTION FOR RELIEF FROM
	) AUTOMATIC STAY 11 U.S.C.
Debtor-in-Possession.	) § 362(d)
	)

Creditor and Moving Party, Children R Us, ("CRU"), alleges as follows:

Creditor is, and at all times herein mentioned was, a California Corporation duly organized and existing under the laws of the State of California.

1.   On or about September 17, 1995 Happy Kids Day Care Center, Inc. ("Happy Kids") filed a petition under Chapter 7 of the Bankruptcy Code.

2.   This Court has jurisdiction over this proceeding pursuant to the process of 28 U.S.C. § 1471 and 11 U.S.C. §§ 361 through 363.

3.   On or about January 12, 1994, Happy Kids, for value received, executed and delivered to CRU, a note and Security Agreement. (Exhibit "A").

4.   The Agreement provides for monthly payments of One Thousand Five Hundred Dollars ($1,500.00) commencing on January 30, 1994 and continue to January 30, 1999, when full payment is due.

5.   The Security interest was granted to CRU on certain personal property described as: (1) Jolly Jumper Swing and Activity Gym, Serial No. JDS 310TN.

6.   The Debtor is in default under the Security Agreement and Creditor is presently entitled to foreclosure upon the personal property.   There is due and owing to Creditor the principal sum of Twelve Thousand Dollars ($12,000.00).

7.   As evidenced by the declaration of John Smith, appraiser, the fair market value of the equipment is Eight Thousand Dollars ($8,000.00).

8.   There is no equity in the personal property for the benefit of the estate.

9.   Creditor's interest in the personal property is without adequate protection pursuant to 11 U.S.C. § 361(d)(1).

WHEREFORE, CREDITOR PRAYS FOR THE FOLLOWING:

1.   That the automatic stay under Section 362 be lifted;

2.   That Debtor be ordered to turnover the personal property to Creditor;

3.   For such other and further relief as this Court deems just and proper.

DATED:_____   _____
                                     Attorneys for Creditor and
                                     Moving Party, Children R Us

FORM 12.3

Declaration of Provable Value

Attorneys for Debtor

UNITED STATES BANKRUPTCY COURT
Southern District of California

In re	)	CASE NO.:95-7654-H11
	)	
HAPPY KIDS DAY CARE CENTER,	)	DECLARATION OF PROVABLE VALUE
Debtor-in-Possession.	)	

I, John Smith declare:

1.   I am an appraiser/auctioneer who has been practicing in the San Diego area for twelve (12) years.

2.   I personally inspected the Jolly Jumper Swing and Activity Gym on September 25, 1996.

3.   The fair market value of the property is Eight Thousand Dollars ($8,000.00).

4.   I also telephoned various used childrens' toy warehouses in the area relative to the fair value of the equipment.

5.   The responses received were in the range of Seven Thousand Eight Hundred Dollars ($7,800.00).

I declare that the foregoing is true and correct.

DATED:_____   _____
                              John Smith

FORM 12.4

**Request for Hearing on Motion for Relief from
Automatic Stay and Notice of Hearing**

UNITED STATES BANKRUPTCY COURT
Southern District of California

In Re

                       Debtor

             Moving Party

            Respondent(s)*

Bankruptcy No.

R.S. Action No.

REQUEST FOR HEARING ON MOTION FOR RELIEF FROM AUTOMATIC STAY
AND NOTICE OF HEARING

TO:*

    YOU ARE NOTIFIED that _____, a party in interest, objects to the above-entitled Motion for Relief From Automatic Stay. Respondent is [check one]:

        [ ] the Debtor   [ ] the Trustee
        [ ] a Creditor   [ ] Other (specify)

    According to the Moving Party's Notice of Filing a Motion for Relief From Automatic Stay, the last date for filing and serving this Request is _____.**

    YOU ARE FURTHER NOTIFIED that a hearing will be held to consider and act upon the Motion in DEPARTMENT _____, United States Bankruptcy Court, Fifth Floor, San Diego, California, on _____, at _____.m.

DATED:_____   _____

                            (Typed Name and Signature)

                            _____

                            (Address)

                            _____

                            City, State and Zip Code)

                            [ ] Attorney for Respondent
                            [ ] Respondent

*Bankruptcy Local Rule 4001-3, printed on the reverse, governs service of this Notice.
Date is calculated as the 11th* day after the day of service of the Notice of Motion, as indicated in the Certification of Service that accompanies that Notice.
***If you were served by mail, the date is calculated as the 14th day after the day of service.

All pleadings related to this RS ACTION must contain the above caption

[Continued on Page 2]

BANKRUPTCY LOCAL RULE 4001-3

"(a) Objections to a motion for relief from stay, together with Local Form CSD 1003, REQUEST FOR HEARING ON MOTION FOR RELIEF FROM AUTOMATIC STAY AND NOTICE OF HEARING, as set forth in Appendix C, shall be served upon the movant and named respondents and the United States Trustee within 11 days from the date of service of the motion for relief from stay and notice. The original and one conformed copy of the pleadings shall likewise be filed with the clerk within the same 11-day period. Bankruptcy Rule 9006(f) shall apply to a motion and objections under this rule.

"(b) Prior to serving the objection, it shall be the duty of the objecting party to obtain from the Court a date and time for hearing on the objections.

Note: For cases filed on or after November 26, 1986, a copy of the motion and notice and subsequent order must be served on the United States Trustee in addition to the other parties required by Bankruptcy Local Rule 4001.

CERTIFICATION OF SERVICE

I, the undersigned whose address appears below, do hereby certify:

1.   That I am, and at all times hereinafter mentioned was, more than 18 years of age.

2.   That on _____ I served a true copy of the within REQUEST FOR HEARING ON MOTION FOR RELIEF FROM AUTOMATIC STAY AND NOTICE OF HEARING, together with a copy of the accompanying DECLARATION IN OPPOSITION TO MOTION FOR RELIEF FROM STAY and [describe any other papers]

by [describe mode of service]:

on [set forth the names and addresses of each person served]:

and, if case filed on or after November 26, 1986, on: United States Trustee
                                                      Department of Justice
                                                      101 W. Broadway, Ste. 440
                                                      San Diego, CA 92101

I hereby certify under penalty of perjury that the foregoing is true and correct.

Executed on_____   _____
                                        (Typed Name and Signature)

                                        _____
                                        (Address)

                                        _____
                                        (City, State and Zip Code)

FORM 18.1

Application to Retain Auctioneer

CSD 244 [Rev.9/89]
Name, Address & Telephone Number

Trustee

UNITED STATES BANKRUPTCY COURT
SOUTHERN DISTRICT OF CALIFORNIA
940 Front Street, Room 5-N-26, San Diego, California 92189

In Re

BANKRUPTCY NO.

Debtor.

APPLICATION TO EMPLOY AUCTIONEER

The application of the undersigned Trustee respectfully represents:

1. Your applicant is the duly appointed and qualified trustee of the estate of the above-named debtor.

2. Your applicant wishes to employ the following named person as Auctioneer in this case: [Name and Address] _____
_____
_____

3. It is necessary to employ an auctioneer because:

4. The property to be sold consists of [general description]:

5. The estimated proceeds from this auction will be $_____

6. The proposed Auctioneer is competent and equipped to perform the auctioneering services required by the estate.

7. In addition to conducting the auction, the proposed Auctioneer will also perform the following services:

8. The Auctioneer has agreed to perform services for $_____[or _____percent of gross sales,] as commission, which amount is reasonable compensation for such services, plus expenses not to exceed the following amount [itemize]:

9. Attached is the verified statement required of the proposed Auctioneer under Local Rule 6005-1.

10. The employment of an Auctioneer to sell the property is in the best interests of the estate and all the creditors.

WHEREFORE, your applicant prays for authorization to employ the Auctioneer named above in paragraph 2 as Auctioneer; that compensation be fixed and expenses be authorized in the amounts shown above in paragraph 8; and for such other and further relief as the Court may deem proper.

Dated:_____   _____, Trustee

CSD 244

145

FORM 18.2

Declaration of Auctioneer

David L. Buchbinder, Esq.
225 Broadway
Suite 1500
San Diego, CA 92101
(619) 233-6993

Trustee in Bankruptcy

UNITED STATES BANKRUPTCY COURT

SOUTHERN DISTRICT OF CALIFORNIA

In re:)   CASE NO.
)
)   DECLARATION OF PROPOSED
)   AUCTIONEER
)
)
        Debtor.   )
_____)

        I, _____, certify and declare as
follows:

        1. I am an Auctioneer licensed to do business in the
County of San Diego, State of California. I maintain an office
within this district located at _____.
I have been requested by DAVID L. BUCHBINDER, ESQ., Trustee in
Bankruptcy herein, to auction property of the estate.

        2. I understand that compensation of my services is
to be subject to the approval of this Court, and I am willing to
conduct the auction and sale under these conditions.

        3. To the best of my knowledge, I represent no interest
adverse to the estate in the matter in which I am to be engaged.

        I certify under penalty of perjury that the foregoing
is true and correct to the best of my knowledge, information and
belief, and that this Declaration was executed on this _____ day
of _____, 1983, at San Diego, California.

                                _____

149

FORM 18.3

Order Appointing Auctioneer

```
UNITED STATES BANKRUPTCY COURT
Southern District of California
```

```
In Re                                    Bankruptcy No.


                    Debtor.
```

ORDER APPOINTING AUCTIONEER

Upon the annexed application of the Trustee in Bankruptcy for the estate of the above-named debtor, praying for authority to employ Auctioneer, and to fix the compensation and expenses of the Auctioneer, and it appearing that no notice of a hearing on the application should be given, and no adverse interest having been represented, and sufficient reason appearing therefor,

IT IS ORDERED that:

1.   The Trustee is authorized to employ _____ as Auctioneer for the Trustee; and

2.   The compensation of said Auctioneer be fixed at $_____, and that expenses are authorized in an amount not to exceed $_____.

3.   Payment to the Auctioneer of the compensation and reimbursement of the expenses herein authorized shall be made only after compliance by the Auctioneer with Bankruptcy Local Rule 6005 and notice to creditors as required by Bankruptcy Local Rule 2002 and 6005-3.

4.   The Trustee serve a copy of the within order on the Auctioneer.

Dated:_____   _____
                               Judge, United States Bankruptcy Court

cc: Trustee

153

FORM 18.4

Notice of Intent to Sell

(2) CSD 226

[Revised August 24, 1983; all prior editions obsolete]
Name, Address and Telephone Number

Trustee
UNITED STATES BANKRUPTCY COURT
SOUTHERN DISTRICT OF CALIFORNIA
940 Front Street, Room 5-N-17   CASE NO. _____
San Diego, California 92189
In re

_____
                                                              Debtor.

NOTICE OF INTENT TO SELL PROPERTY OF ESTATE AT PUBLIC SALE

TO: THE DEBTOR, HIS CREDITORS, AND INTERESTED PARTIES:

    You are hereby notified:

    1.   That _____, the trustee herein,
proposes to sell the following property of the estate at public sale [general description]:

    2.   A copy of the inventory and/or full description of the property to be sold may be
obtained by calling the office of the trustee at the telephone number shown above.
    3.   To the best of my knowledge, these items are free of any encumbrance or, if an encumb-
rance is known, the encumbrance will be paid in full from the proceeds of sale of this property
or in accordance with further order of the court.

    4.   The sale will be held on _____, at _____.m.,
at the following location:

    5.   The property to be sold will be available for viewing at the place of sale on

_____ between _____.m and _____.m.

    If you object to the proposed action, YOU ARE REQUIRED:

    1.   To obtain a hearing date and time from the Courtroom Deputy for Bankruptcy Judge

_____, by calling Telephone Number (619) 293-_____;

    2.   WITHIN 20 DAYS FROM THE DATE OF SERVICE OF THIS NOTICE OF MOTION [OR INTENT], to serve
a copy of your Declaration in Opposition to the proposed action and a separate Request for
and Notice of Hearing* upon the undersigned [attorney for the] moving party, and to file the
original and one copy of the papers and proof of service with the Clerk of the United States
Bankruptcy Court, at 940 Front Street, Room 5-N-17, San Diego, California 92189.

    Any opposing declaration to the proposed action shall be signed and verified in the manner
prescribed by Bankruptcy Rule 9011, and the declaration shall:
    (1) identify the interest of the opposing party; and
    (2) state with particularity the grounds for the opposition.

    You are further notified that IF YOU FAIL TO REQUEST AND SERVE NOTICE OF A HEARING and your
opposing declaration within the 20 day period provided by this notice, the undersigned will
proceed to take the proposed action without further notice to you or a hearing.

    Dated:
                                    _____
                                                   Trustee

[Insert Date of Service]: _____

*You may obtain Form CSD 118, "Request for and Notice of Hearing" from the Clerk of Court at the
address stated herein.

CSD 226

FORM 18.5

Report of Sale

UNITED STATES BANKRUPTCY COURT
Southern District of California

In Re	Bankruptcy No.
Debtor.	

REPORT OF SALE

Pursuant to Bankruptcy Local Rule 6004, the undersigned Trustee hereby reports and represents:

1. On _____, due notice of the trustee's intent to sell the property described herein was mailed to the debtor and debtor's attorney and all creditors as required by Bankruptcy Local Rules 2002 and 6004.

2. The time for filing a request for hearing has expired without an objection or request for hearing having been received by the undersigned.

3. A description of the property sold, name of the purchaser(s), and the terms of sale are set forth in Exhibit "A" printed on page 2.

4. If applicable, the following entities held a valid security interest in all or part of the property sold and were paid the stated sums in satisfaction thereof:

Name and Address	Property	Amount Paid

5. The purchase price has been paid in full and all property delivered to the purchaser.

I hereby declare under penalty of perjury that the within and attached statements are true to the best of my knowledge.

DATED:_____   _____
                                       Trustee in Bankruptcy

[Continued on Page 2]

_____DEBTOR, CASE NO._____

Type of Sale:[1]

[ ] Private Sale. Describe methods used to obtain best possible price:[2]

Description of   Name and Address   Sales Price per
Property Sold   of Purchaser(s)   Item or Lot

     Offers or bids received but not accepted from the following entities:

     Name   Value of Offer

[ ] Public Auction. Auction conducted by_____

Report of Auctioneer attached containing:[3]

     List of the names of bidders and assigned bidding numbers, if any; and

     -     Description of items sold, purchase price, and name or bidder
           number for purchaser for each item or lot sold; plus

     -     A cover page containing a summation of the gross sales, and a
           statement of the commission and expenses applied for or retained
           by the auctioneer.

           A statement that there was at the time of employment, and continued
           to be during the period of employment, a disinterested person as
           required under 11 U.S.C. § 327, or, if so, the nature thereof.

                 Auctioneer's Report Reviewed and Approved:

                 Signed:_____, Trustee

_____
INSTRUCTIONS:

     _____

          [1] Indicate method of sale, whether by sealed bids,
     negotiations or otherwise.

          [2] Describe advertising, telephone or other forms of
     solicitation for offers, negotiations and any other methods used
     to consummate sale.

          [3] Auctioneer's report to be signed under penalty of perjury,
     contain all of the information here set forth, and to be reviewed
     and approved by trustee.

162

FORM 20.1

Report of Abandonment

UNITED STATES BANKRUPTCY COURT
Southern District of California

In Re

Bankruptcy No.

Debtor.

REPORT OF ABANDONMENT OF REAL PROPERTY

Pursuant to Bankruptcy Local Rule 6007, the undersigned Trustee hereby reports and represents:

1.   On _____, due notice of the trustee's intent to abandon the property described herein was mailed to the debtor and debtor's attorney and such other parties as required by Bankruptcy Local Rule 6007.

2.   The time for filing a request for hearing has expired without an objection or request for hearing having been received by the undersigned.

3.   The trustee hereby abandons and forever disclaims any further interest in and to the following described real property of the debtor herein, to wit: (Provide full legal description and street address - use continuation sheet if necessary):

4.   Right of possession of the abandoned property is hereby relinquished to the debtor, to be assumed at no cost to the undersigned. Said abandonment is subject to and without prejudice to any rights of any entity holding a valid lien against the property or of any right of redemption that may be exercised by the debtor under 11 U.S.C. § 722.

On this date I caused a copy of this Report to be mailed to the debtor and debtor's attorney of record, and to the following parties in interest [continued on reverse, if needed]:

I hereby declare under penalty of perjury that the foregoing statements are true to the best of my knowledge and belief.

DATED:_____   _____
                                         Signature of the Trustee

165

FORM 21.1

Proof of Claim

B10 (Official Form 10)
(Rev. 6/91)

United States Bankruptcy Court ——————— District of ————————	PROOF OF CLAIM
In re (Name of Debtor)	Case Number

NOTE This form should not be used to make a claim for an administrative expense arising after the commencement of the case A "request" of payment of an administrative expense may be filed pursuant to 11 U.S.C. § 503.

Name of Creditor *(The person or entity to whom the debtor owes money or property)* Name and Addresses Where Notices Should be Sent Telephone No.	☐ Check box if you are aware that anyone else has filed a proof of claim relating to your claim. Attach copy of statement giving particulars. ☐ Check box if you have never received any notices from the bankruptcy court in this case. ☐ Check box if the address differs from the address on the envelope sent to you by the court.	THIS SPACE IS FOR COURT USE ONLY

ACCOUNT OR OTHER NUMBER BY WHICH CREDITOR IDENTIFIES DEBTOR	Check here if this claim: ☐ replaces ☐ amends a previously filed claim, dated ———————

1. BASIS FOR CLAIM

☐ Goods sold
☐ Services performed
☐ Money loaned
☐ Personal injury/wrongful death
☐ Taxes
☐ Other (Describe briefly)

☐ Retiree benefits as defined in 11 U.S.C § 1114(a)
☐ Wages, salaries, and compensations (Fill out below)
Your social security number _____
Unpaid compensations for services performed
from _____ to _____
        (date)   (date)

2 DATE DEBT WAS INCURRED	3. IF COURT JUDGMENT, DATE OBTAINED

4. CLASSIFICATION OF CLAIM Under the Bankruptcy Code all claims are classified as one or more of the following (1) Unsecured nonpriority, (2) Unsecured Priority (3) Secured. It is possible for part of a claim to be in one category and part in another CHECK THE APPROPRIATE BOX OR BOXES that best describe your claim and STATE THE AMOUNT OF THE CLAIM.

☐ SECURED CLAIM $ _____
Attach evidence of perfection of security interest
Brief Description of Collateral
☐ Real Estate   ☐ Motor Vehicle   ☐ Other (Describe briefly)

Amount of arrearage and other charges included in secured claim above,
if any $ _____

☐ UNSECURED NONPRIORITY CLAIM $ _____
A claim is unsecured if there is no collateral or lien on property of the debtor securing the claim or to the extent that the value of such property is less than the amount of the claim.

☐ UNSECURED PRIORITY CLAIM $ _____
Specify the priority of the claim.

☐ Wages, salaries, or commissions (up to $2000), earned not more than 90 days before filing of the bankruptcy petition or cessation of the debtor's business, whichever is earlier)—11 U.S.C § 507(a)(3)
☐ Contributions to an employee benefit plan—U.S.C. § 507(a)(4)
☐ Up to $900 of deposits toward purchase, lease, or rental of property or services for personal, family, or household use—11 U.S.C. § 507(a)(6)
☐ Taxes or penalties of governmental units—11 U.S.C. § 507(a)(7)
☐ Other—11 U.S.C. §§ 507(a)(2), (a)(5)—(Describe briefly)

5 TOTAL AMOUNT OF CLAIM AT TIME CASE FILED:
$ _____ (Unsecured) $ _____ (Secured) $ _____ (Priority) $ _____ (Total)

☐ Check this box if claim includes prepetition charges in addition to the principal amount of the claim. Attach itemized statement of all additional charges

6 CREDITS AND SETOFFS The amount of all payments on this claim has been credited and deducted for the purpose of making this proof of claim. In filing this claim, claimant has deducted all amounts that claimant owes to debtor.

7 SUPPORTING DOCUMENTS *Attach copies of supporting documents,* such as promissory notes, purchase orders, invoices, itemized statements of running accounts, contracts, court judgments, or evidence of security interests. If the documents are not available, explain. If the documents are voluminous, attach a summary.

8 TIME-STAMPED COPY To receive an acknowledgement of the filing of your claim, enclose a stamped, self-addressed envelope and copy of this proof of claim.

THIS SPACE IS FOR
COURT USE ONLY

Date	Sign and print the name and title, if any, of the creditor or other person authorized to file this claim (attach copy of power of attorney, if any)

Penalty for presenting fraudulent claim: Fine of up to $500,000 or imprisonment for up to 5 years, or both. 18 U.S.C. §§ 152 and 3571.

FORM 21.2

Objection to Claim and Notice Thereof

CSD 2015 [6/01/93]
Name, Address, Telephone No. & I.D. No.

UNITED STATES BANKRUPTCY COURT
SOUTHERN DISTRICT OF CALIFORNIA
940 Front Street, Room 5-N-26, San Diego, California 92189-0020

In Re

Tax I.D.#:	BANKRUPTCY NO.
Social Security #:	Debtor.

OBJECTION TO CLAIM AND NOTICE THEREOF

TO:

The [ ] Trustee [ ] Debtor [ ] Chapter 13 Trustee, except to the extent already paid by the Chapter 13 trustee, objects to the allowance of Claim No._____, by _____, filed for S_____, on the grounds it:

   [ ] Duplicates Claim No._____ filed by _____.

   [ ] The claim was filed after the expiration of the last date to file claims.

   [ ] Does not include an itemized statement of the account.

   [ ] Does not include a copy of the underlying judgment.

   [ ] Does not include a copy of the security agreement and evidence of perfection.

   [ ] Does not include a copy of the writing upon which it is based.

For the following objections, attach affidavits or declarations in accordance with Bankruptcy Local Rule 9013-2(a)(4).:

   [ ] Fails to assert grounds for priority.

   [ ] Appears to include interest or charges accrued after the filing of this case on _____.

   [ ] Other [State grounds and cite applicable Code section or case authority.]:

If you object to the proposed action:

1.   **YOU ARE REQUIRED** to obtain a hearing date and time from the appropriate Courtroom Deputy for the judge assigned to your bankruptcy case. If a Chapter 7, 11, or 12 case, determine which deputy to call by looking at the Bankruptcy Case No. ir the above caption of this notice. If the case number is followed by the letter(s):

-	M	-	call	(619) 557-6019 -	DEPARTMENT ONE
-	A	-	call	(619) 557-6594 -	DEPARTMENT TWO
-	H	-	call	(619) 557-6018 -	DEPARTMENT THREE
-	B	-	call	(619) 557-5157 -	DEPARTMENT FOUR

For ALL Chapter 13 cases, call (619) 557-5955.

CSD 2015

[Continued on Page 2]

2.   **WITHIN THIRTY (30)¹ DAYS FROM THE DATE OF SERVICE OF THIS MOTION,** you are further required to serve a copy of your DECLARATION IN OPPOSITION TO MOTION and separate REQUEST AND NOTICE OF HEARING [Local Form CSD 1184²] upon the undersigned moving party, together with any opposing papers. The opposing declaration shall be signed and verified in the manner prescribed by Federal Rule of Bankruptcy Procedure 9011, and the declaration shall:

      a.   identify the interest of the opposing party; and

      b.   state, with particularity, the grounds for the opposition.

3.   **YOU MUST** file the original and one copy of the Declaration and Request and Notice of Hearing with proof of service with the Clerk of the U.S. Bankruptcy Court at 940 Front Street, Room 5-N-26, San Diego, California 92189-0020, no later than the next business day following the date of service.

IF YOU FAIL TO SERVE YOUR "DECLARATION IN OPPOSITION TO INTENDED ACTION" AND "REQUEST AND NOTICE OF HEARING" within the 30-day¹ period provided by this notice, NO HEARING SHALL TAKE PLACE, you shall lose your opportunity for hearing, and the debtor or trustee may proceed to take the intended action.

DATED: _____   _____

                                       Trustee [Debtor]

CERTIFICATE OF SERVICE

I, the undersigned whose address appears below, certify:

That I am, and at all times hereinafter mentioned was, more than 18 years of age;

That on _____ day of _____, 19_____, I served a true copy of the within OBJECTION TO CLAIM AND NOTICE THEREOF by [describe here mode of service]

on the following persons [set forth name and address of each person served] and as checked below:

[ ]   For Chpt. 7, 11, & 12 cases: [ ] For Chpt. 13 cases numbered   [ ] For Chpt. 13 cases numbered
                                                 90-08445 or lower and ODD   90-08446 to 92-01215 and EVEN
        UNITED STATES TRUSTEE   numbers beginning with 92-01217:   numbers beginning with 92-01216:
        Department of Justice   BARRY W. HEID, TRUSTEE   DAVID L. SKELTON, TRUSTEE
        101 West Broadway, Suite 440   Post Office Box 671   620 "C" Street, Suite 413
        San Diego, CA 92101   San Diego, CA 92112   San Diego, CA 92112-5312

        I certify under penalty of perjury that the foregoing is true and correct.

        Executed on _____   _____
                    (Date)   (Typed Name and Signature)

                                                      _____
                                                      (Address)

                                                      _____
                                                      (City, State, ZIP Code)

¹If you were served by mail, you have three (3) additional days to take the above-stated actions.
²You may obtain Local Form CSD 1184 from the Office of the Clerk of the U.S. Bankruptcy Court.

CSD 2015

FORM 21.3

Statement of Intention

UNITED STATES BANKRUPTCY COURT
DISTRICT OF _____

In re_____,
                             Debtor

Case No._____

Chapter Seven

CHAPTER 7 INDIVIDUAL DEBTOR'S STATEMENT OF INTENTION

1. I, the debtor, have filed a schedule of assets and liabilities which includes consumer debts secured by property of the estate.

2. My intention with respect to the property of the estate which secures those consumer debts is as follows:

      a. *Property to Be Surrendered.*

Description of Property	Creditor's Name
1. _____	_____
2. _____	_____
3. _____	_____

      b. *Property to Be Retained. [Check applicable statement of debtor's intention concerning reaffirmation, redemption, or lien avoidance.]*

Description of Property	Creditor's name	Debt will be reaffirmed pursuant to § 524(c)	Property is claimed as exempt and will be redeemed pursuant to § 722	Lien will be avoided pursuant to § 522(f) and property will be claimed as exempt
1. _____	_____	_____	_____	_____
2. _____	_____	_____	_____	_____
3. _____	_____	_____	_____	_____
4. _____	_____	_____	_____	_____
5. _____	_____	_____	_____	_____

3. I understand that § 521(2)(B) of the Bankruptcy Code requires that I perform the above stated intention within 45 days of the filing of this statement with the court, or within such additional time as the court, for cause, within such 45-day period fixes.

Date: _____

_____
Signature of Debtor

Forms Inc. • P.O. Box 1109 • La Jolla, CA 92038 • 800/854-1080 • Official Form 8

FORM 23.1

Chapter 13 Plan

UNITED STATES BANKRUPTCY COURT
SOUTHERN DISTRICT OF CALIFORNIA

In re: Chapter 13 DEBTORS PLAN

                                                                    Case No.

There shall be paid to the Chapter 13 Trustee $ each month by debtor(s), or any entity from whom
debtor(s) receive income, in such installments as agreed upon with the Trustee, for payment of all existing
debts of debtor(s) pursuant to this Plan, except as the court may otherwise order. Debtor(s) submit all future
income to the supervision and control of trustee during the pendency of this case and agree to pay sufficient
funds to the Trustee on or before five years from commencement of this case to fully complete this Plan.

1.   Administrative Claims. Trustee shall disburse dividends to all section 1326(a) claims and charges in
advance of all other claims, unless priority expressly waived. All other section 1322(a) and section 1305(a)
(1) claims allowed shall be paid in full by deferred payments in such priority and installments as the trustee
in his sole discretion deems appropriate.

2.   Unsecured Claims. After dividends to other creditors pursuant to this Plan, trustee shall pay dividends
prorata on claims allowed unsecured herein to   of the amount allowed in full satisfaction thereof. (If
left blank, pay 100%).

3.   Secured Claims, Personal Property. After payments provided for by Paragraph 1 of this Plan, trustee
shall make payment to creditors named in this paragraph whose claims are allowed secured solely by personal
property. Each named creditor shall be paid in installments from funds available for distribution monthly, non-
cumulative, as indicated until claim in amount filed and allowed plus interest at ten (10%) percent per annum
is paid.

Name of Creditor   Fair Value   Installment

Holders of claims allowed as secured solely by personal property, other than named above, shall be paid
dividends prorata with other such creditors to the amount allowed secured plus interest at ten (10%) percent
per annum and in advance of distribution to general unsecured creditors. Any creditor holding a lease on
personal property in debtors possession who files a claim herein and does not expressly reject this Plan, unless
otherwise specifically dealt with by this Plan, shall be treated as a secured creditor.

4.   Secured Creditors, Real Estate. Except as the court may otherwise order, debtor(s) during the pendency
of this case shall make, and following completion of this case shall continue to make, the usual and regular
payments called for by any security agreements supporting non-voidable liens against debtor(s) real estate
directly to each of said lienholders in a current manner. However,

Arrearages to named lienholders (their agents or assigns) shall be paid in installments by trustee from
funds available for distribution monthly, non-cumulative, and, except for creditors specifically named in
Paragraph 3 of this Plan, shall be paid in advance of periodic distribution to other creditors. Payments shall
be made in installments set forth below until amount allowed each lienholder on a claim for arrearages filed
herein has been paid:

Lienholder   Arrearages   Installment

Provisions of this Paragraph shall operate to cure any default of any real estate security agreement
notwithstanding that by the terms thereof or by the laws or processes of a governmental unit the time for
redemption or reinstatement has expired.

Notwithstanding any other provision of this Paragraph, if debtor(s) fail to make payment to the trustee
as provided by this Plan, any funds held by trustee may be distributed to creditors other than those provided
for by this Paragraph.

If there exist creditors not named in this Paragraph holding statutory or other liens against debtors
real estate and the obligation is fully due, for reasons other than exercise of a power of acceleration for
failure to make installment payments, unless the court under Section 362(d) orders otherwise, debtor(s) will

1/1/83   Page 1 of

181

pay said claim directly to said creditor in full on or before six months time following the date of confirmation of this Plan.

5.   Lien Avoidance. Debtor(s) hereby elect to avoid the fixing of liens pursuant to Section 522(f), Bankruptcy Code. All secured creditors, except those whose liens are avoidable pursuant to the provisions of Section 522(f), shall retain their liens until paid as provided for by this Plan.

6.   Rejection of Claim, Secured Creditor. Debtor(s) elect not to assume the lease or contract with creditor(s) named in this Paragraph and shall surrender to such creditor the collateral subject to creditors lien or lease in full satisfaction of any and all claims, secured or unsecured, creditor may have against debtor(s) arising from the transaction creating creditors interest in the said property: (name creditors)

7.   Exclusion of Creditor. Notwithstanding any other provisions of this Plan, debtor(s) elect to assume the existing lease or contract with creditors named in this Paragraph. These named creditors shall not be dealt with or provided for by this Plan: (name creditors)

8.   Post-petition Claims. Claims allowed for post-petition debts incurred by debtor(s) may be paid in full and in such order and on such terms as the trustee, in his sole discretion, may determine. Trustee may file to dismiss case if debtor(s) incur post-petition debts without the written consent of trustee and debtor(s) fail to keep such obligations current in payment.

9.   General Provisions. If this case is filed as a joint debtor case, the debtors' estates shall be fully consolidated for purposes of administration. Pursuant to Section 1322(b)(3), Bankruptcy Code, trustee shall have the power to waive, in writing and on such conditions as the trustee may impose, any default in debtor(s) payment to trustee under this Plan.

Plan dated:_____   _____
                                      Debtor

                                      _____
                                      Debtor

1/1/83   Page 2 of

182

FORM 23.2

Chapter 13 Notice to Creditors

IN RE:

CHAPTER 13 CASE NUMBER
9304220 H   13

SSN(1
SSN(2):000-00-0000

92129-0000

AKA(1
AKA(2,

DBA(1):
DBA(2):

Order and Notice for Meeting of Creditors
To Be Held on Jun 11, 1993 At 9:00 AM

An order for relief under Chapter 13 of Title 11 of the United States Code was
entered on Apr 22, 1993 upon filing of a petition by the above debtor(s). As a
result of the filing, certain acts and proceedings against debtor and debtor's
property are stayed as provided in 11 USC 362(a) and against certain codebtors
as provided in 11 USC 1301. Notice is given that a Meeting of Creditors under
11 USC 341(a) shall be held on Jun 11, 1993 at 9:00 AM at 620 C STREET
SUITE 400   ,SAN DIEGO CA, 92101. Debtor(s) shall appear for examinatio
and you may attend the meeting for that purpose. The meeting may thereafter be
continued without further written notice. If debtor(s) fails to appear at the
scheduled 341(a) meeting, the Trustee or U.S. Trustee will move for dismissal
of this case without further notice to the debtor or creditors. In order to
have a claim allowed and participate in the distribution of any dividend, A
CREDITOR MUST FILE A CLAIM, even if the creditor is not on the list of creditors
filed by the debtor(s). CLAIMS WHICH ARE NOT FILED BY Sep 9, 1993 WILL NOT BE
ALLOWED EXCEPT AS PROVIDED BY LAW.

A hearing on confirmation of the plan will be held ONLY IF WRITTEN OBJECTIONS TO
CONFIRMATION (FORM CSD 1172) AND NOTICE OF HEARING THEREON (FORM CSD 1173) ARE
TIMELY FILED WITH CLERK, BANKRUPTCY COURT, PURSUANT TO RULE 3015 LOCAL
BANKRUPTCY RULES. IF NONE SO FILED, PROPOSED PLAN MAY BE CONFIRMED WITHOUT
FURTHER NOTICE AND CONFIRMED PLAN WILL BE BINDING ON ALL CREDITORS. NOTICE IS
ALSO GIVEN THAT COURT MAY GRANT DEBTORS ATTORNEY FEES IN EXCESS OF $500 UNLESS
WRITTEN OBJECTION IS FILED PRIOR TO THE END OF THE SECTION 341(a) HEARING.

The plan proposes payments of $ 500.00 per month to the Trustee, and will pay
a 100.00% dividend to unsecured creditors over a plan length of approximately
 60 months. Unsecured claims to be paid   .00 percent A.P.R. interest.
Creditors allowed secured other than real estate creditors to be paid 10% APR
interest on amount allowed secured and in advance of general unsecured claims.

FILE CLAIM IN DUPLICATE WITH: DATED: Apr 27, 1993 BY THE COURT
U.S. BANKRUPTCY COURT   BARRY K. LANDER, CLERK
C/O DAVID L. SKELTON, TRUSTEE   940 FRONT STREET
620 "C" STREET, SUITE 413   5TH FLOOR, ROOM 5-N-26
SAN DIEGO, CA   SAN DIEGO, CA   92189-0020
           92101-5312

ATTORNEY FOR DEBTOR:(619)236-1741   SCHEDULED DEBTS:
     MARK RICHARD NIMS, ESQ   SECURED   PRIORITY   UNSECURED
     501 W BROADWAY #720   17,520.00   .00   6,118.00
     SAN DIEGO CA
              92101-0000

IN RE: CHAPTER 13 CASE NUMBER
                                          9304220 H 13

                                          SSN(1
                                          SSN(2):000-00-0000
                     92129-0000
AKA(1)   DBA(1):
AKA(2)   DBA(2):

                    FIRST MEETING ADDITIONAL INFORMATION

        Debtors Chapter 13 plan is on file at the Bankruptcy Court and is a
public record. Creditors must refer to the plan for precise details.

Special Notice to AZTEC HOME LOAN   at $ 475.00 per month.

Real Estate Claims -- Debtor proposes to make regular monthly payments to lien
holders directly -- However arrears on liens to be paid through the plan in
non-cumulative installments indicated above.

Special Notice to FORD MOTOR CREDIT
Collateral: LEASED 1993 HONDA

Excluded Claims -- Debtors elect to assume the existing lease or contract with
creditors named above. These named creditors shall not be dealt with or
provided for by this plan.

FORM 24.1

Chapter 11 Monthly Operating Report

Attorney for Debtor-in-Possession

UNITED STATES BANKRUPTCY COURT
SOUTHERN DISTRICT OF CALIFORNIA

In re:)   CASE NUMBER
)
)   DEBTOR-IN-POSSESSION
)   MONTHLY OPERATING
)   REPORT FOR THE MONTH OF
)   _____, 19 ___
)
)
)
)
                   Debtor(s)   )
_____   )

TO: THE HONORABLE _____
      UNITED STATES BANKRUPTCY JUDGE

The Debtor-in-Possession hereby files its monthly Operating
Report pursuant to the United States Trustee's Operating and
Reporting Requirements for Chapter 11 cases.

DATED: _____
                                    Attorney for Debtor-in-Possession

189

```
┌─────────────────────────────────────────────┐
│  UNITED STATES DEPARTMENT OF JUSTICE          │
│  OFFICE OF THE UNITED STATES TRUSTEE          │
└─────────────────────────────────────────────┘
```

┌──────────────────────────────────┐
│ In re: │   CHAPTER 11 (BUSINESS)
│   │
│   │   CASE NO. _____
│   │
│   │   OPERATING REPORT NO. _____
│   Debtor(s)   │   FROM: _____
└──────────────────────────────────┘   TO: _____

RECEIPTS AND DISBURSEMENTS

[GENERAL ACCOUNT]

__CASH ACTIVITY*__

A. Total Receipts per all prior General Account Reports $_____
B. Less: Total Disbursements per all prior General
           Account Reports $_____
C. Beginning Balance: (A minus B) $_____
D. Receipts During Current Period:
        Accounts Receivable - Pre-filing $_____
        Accounts Receivable - Post-filing $_____
        General Sales $_____
        Other (specify) _____ $_____
        Other** (specify) _____ $_____

                        TOTAL RECEIPTS THIS PERIOD $_____

E. Balance (C + D): $_____
F. Less: Disbursements During Current Period
           (Attach separate listing if needed)

    Date   Check No.   Payee   Purpose   Amount

                    TOTAL DISBURSEMENTS THIS PERIOD: $_____

G. ENDING BALANCE (E minus F) $_____
                                                      =============
H. General Account Number _____
    Depository Name and Location _____
    _____

*   All receipts coming into the estate must be deposited in the general
    account.

** Sale of any real or personal property out of the ordinary course of
    business; attach exhibit specifying what was sold, to whom, terms
    and date of court order or report of sale.

RECEIPTS AND DISBURSEMENTS

[PAYROLL ACCOUNT]

A. Total Receipts per all prior
    Payroll Account Reports $_____

B. Less: Total Disbursements per all prior
           Payroll Account Reports $_____

C. Beginning Balance (A minus B) $_____

D. Receipts:
    Transferred from General Account $_____

E. Balance (C + D) $_____

F. Less: Disbursements During Current Period

    Date   Check No.   Payee   Amount

                    TOTAL DISBURSEMENTS THIS PERIOD: $_____

G. ENDING BALANCE (E minus F) $_____
                                                      ============

H. Payroll Account Number _____
    Depository Name and Location _____
    _____

191

RECEIPTS AND DISBURSEMENTS

[TAX ACCOUNT]

A. Total Receipts per all prior
    Tax Account Reports $_____

B. Less: Total Disbursements per all prior
           Tax Account Reports $_____

C. Beginning Balance (A minus B) $_____

D. Receipts:
    Transferred from General Account $_____

                    TOTAL RECEIPTS THIS PERIOD $_____

E. Balance (C + D): $_____

F. Less: Disbursements During Current Period

Date	Check No.	Payee	Purpose	Amount

                TOTAL DISBURSEMENTS THIS PERIOD: $_____

G. ENDING BALANCE (E minus F) $_____
                                                         ===============

H. Tax Account Number _____
    Depository Name and Location _____

SUMMARY SCHEDULE OF CASH

Ending Balance for Period:

    General Account $_____
    Payroll Account $_____
    Tax Account $_____
    Other Accounts - Specify
    _____ $_____
    Other Monies - Specify
    (i.e., CD, investment
     securities, etc.)
    _____ $_____
    Petty Cash* $_____

    TOTAL CASH AVAILABLE $===============

* Attach exhibit itemizing all petty cash transactions.

192

STATUS OF PAYMENTS TO SECURED CREDITORS, LESSORS AND OTHER PARTIES TO EXECUTORY CONTRACTS

Creditor, Etc.	Frequency of Payments (i.e. mo.,qtr.)	Amount of Payment	Post-Petition Payments not made Number	Total Due

TAX LIABILITY
(Post-Petition Cash Basis)

For the Reporting Period:
Gross Sales Subject to Sales Tax $_____

Total Wages Paid $_____

	Post-Petition Amts Paid	Post-Petition Amts Owing	Post-Petition Amts Delinquent
Federal Withholding			
State Withholding			
FICA - Employer's Share			
FICA - Employees' Share			
Federal Unemployment			
State Unemployment			
Sales and Use			
Real Property			
Other: (Specify)			
_____			
TOTALS			

AGING OF ACCOUNTS PAYABLE AND ACCOUNTS RECEIVABLE

	ACCOUNTS PAYABLE* (Post-Petition only)	ACCOUNTS RECEIVABLE Pre-Petition	Post-Petition
30 days or less	$		
31-60 days	$		
61-90 days	$		
91-120 days	$		
Over 120 days	$		
TOTALS	$		

UNITED STATES TRUSTEE QUARTERLY FEES
(Total Payments)

Qtrly Period Ending	Total Disbursements	Qtrly Fee	Date Paid	Amount Paid	Qtrly Fee Still Owing

* Attach exhibit listing and aging all accounts payable owing for payroll and utilities.

194

PROFIT AND LOSS STATEMENT
(Accrual Basis Only)

	Current Month	Cumulative Post-Petition
Sales:		
Gross Sales	_____	_____
Less: Returns/Discounts	(_____)	(_____)
Net Sales	_____	_____
Cost of Goods Sold:		
Beginning Inventory at cost	_____	_____
Purchases	_____	_____
Less: Ending Inventory at cost	(_____)	(_____)
Cost of Goods Sold (COGS)	_____	_____
Gross Profit (Net Sales Less COGS)	_____	_____
Other Operating Income (Itemize)	_____	_____
Operating Expenses:		
Officer/Mgmt Payroll	_____	_____
Payroll - Other Employees	_____	_____
Payroll Taxes	_____	_____
Other Taxes (Itemize)	_____	_____
Depreciation and Amortization	_____	_____
Rental - Real Property	_____	_____
Leases - Personal Property	_____	_____
Insurance	_____	_____
Telephone and Utilities	_____	_____
Repairs and Maintenance	_____	_____
Travel and Entertainment (Itemize)	_____	_____
Misc. Operating Expenses (Itemize)	_____	_____
Total Operating Expenses	(_____)	(_____)
Net Gain/(Loss) from Operations	_____	_____
Non-Operating Income:		
Interest Income	_____	_____
Net Gain on Sale of Assets (Itemize)	_____	_____
Other (Itemize)	_____	_____
Total Non-Operating Income	_____	_____
Non-Operating Expenses:		
Interest Expense	_____	_____
Legal and Professional (Itemize)	_____	_____
Other (Itemize)	_____	_____
Total Non-Operating Expenses	(_____)	(_____)
NET INCOME/(LOSS)	_____	_____

*Attach exhibit listing all itemizations required above.

INSURANCE COVERAGE

	Name of Carrier	Amount of Coverage	Policy Expiration Date	Premium Paid Through Date
General Liability				
Workers Compensation				
Casualty				
Vehicle				
Other (Specify): _____				
_____				

QUESTIONNAIRE

Has the Debtor-in-Possession made any payments on its pre-petition unsecured debt, except as have been authorized by the Court?

_____Yes; Explain _____

_____No

Has the Debtor-in-Possession during this reporting period provided compensation or remuneration to any officers, directors, principals or other insiders without appropriate authorization?

_____Yes; Amount, to whom and for what period _____

_____

_____No

I, (Name, Title)_____, have fully read and understood the foregoing Debtor-in-Possession Operating Report and declare under penalty of perjury that the information enclosed herein is true and complete to the best of my knowledge.

DATED:_____   _____
                                      Principal for Debtor-in-Possession

196

FORM 24.2

Exhibit "A" to Voluntary Petition

UNITED STATES BANKRUPTCY COURT

_____ **District of** _____

In re _____

                                    Debtor

Case No. _____

Chapter_____

Exhibit "A" to Voluntary Petition

1. Debtor's employer identification number is_____ .

2. If any of debtor's securities are registered under section 12 of the Securities and Exchange Act of 1934, the SEC file number is _____ .

3. The following financial data is the latest available information and refers to debtor's condition on _____ .

		Approximate number of holders
a. Total assets	$_____	
b. Total liabilities	$_____	
Fixed, liquidated secured debt	$_____	_____
Contingent secured debt	$_____	_____
Disputed secured claims	$_____	_____
Unliquidated secured debt	$_____	_____

		Approximate number of holders
Fixed, liquidated unsecured debt	$_____	_____
Contingent unsecured debt	$_____	_____
Disputed unsecured claims	$_____	_____
Unliquidated unsecured debt	$_____	_____
Number of shares of preferred stock	_____	_____
Number of shares of common stock	_____	_____

Forms Inc. • P.O. Box 1109 • La Jolla, CA 92038-1109 • (800) 854-1080 • Official Form 1 - Exhibit A(1)

Exhibit "A" continued

Comments, if any: _____
_____
_____
_____

4. Brief description of debtor's business:_____
_____
_____

5. List the name of any person who directly or indirectly owns, controls, or holds, with power to vote, 20 % or more of the voting securities of debtor:_____
_____
_____
_____

6. List the names of all corporations 20% or more of the outstanding voting securities of which are directly or indirectly owned, controlled, or hled, with power to vote, by debtor:_____
_____
_____
_____

DECLARATION UNDER PENALTY OF PERJURY
ON BEHALF OF A CORPORATION OR PARTNERSHIP

I, [the president *or* other officer *or* an authorized agent of the corporation] [*or* a member *or* an authorized agent of the partnership] named as the debtor in this case, declare under penalty of perjury that I have read the foregoing Exhibit "A" and that it is true and correct to the best of my information and belief.

Date_____

Signature_____

_____
(Print Name and Title)

Forms Inc. • P.O. Box 1109 • La Jolla, CA 92038-1109 • (800) 854-1080 • Official Form 1 - Exhibit A(2)

FORM 26.1

Chapter 11 Notice of Confirmation Hearing

Attorneys for Debtor-In-Possession

UNITED STATES BANKRUPTCY COURT

SOUTHERN DISTRICT OF CALIFORNIA

In re   )   CASE NO. 88-8888-Z11
)
JOHN SMITH,   )   NOTICE OF TIME FOR FILING
)   ACCEPTANCES OR REJECTIONS
)   OF PLAN, OF TIME OF
)   HEARING ON CONFIRMATION,
             Debtor-in-Possession.   )   AND OF TIME FOR FILING
)   OBJECTIONS TO CONFIRMATION
)
)   DATE: MAY 10, 1989
)   TIME: 9:30 A.M.
)   DEPT: 2
_____)

TO: ALL CREDITORS AND PARTIES IN INTEREST:

1.   On or about March 17, 1989, the Court entered its Order approving Debtor's Disclosure Statement.   This Disclosure Statement, filed March 9, 1989, was filed in connection with the Debtor's Plan of Reorganization.

2.   There is transmitted herewith:

(a) A copy of Debtor's Plan of Reorganization;

(b) A copy of Debtor's approved Disclosure Statement;

(c) A copy of the Order Approving the Disclosure Statement; and

(d) Appropriate forms for the acceptance or rejection of the Plan of Reorganization ("Plan").

3.   Pursuant to Local Bankruptcy Rules of Procedure, Rules

3017 and 3018, acceptance or rejection of the Plan may be filed in writing by the holders of all claims in interest impaired by said Plan on or before May 1, 1989.

4. Appropriate forms for the acceptance or rejection of the Plan are enclosed for the convenience of the holders of claims or interest, if they desire to accept or reject said Plan. Other forms may be obtained from the undersigned upon request, or from the Court.

5. Any objections to the confirmation of the Plan must be filed with the Court and served upon Debtor's counsel on or before May 3, 1989, ten (10) days prior to the date of this hearing.

7. A hearing for consideration of the confirmation of the Plan will be held on May 10, 1989 at 9:30 a.m. in Department 2 located at the United States Bankruptcy Court, 940 Front Street, Fifth Floor, San Diego, California.

DOE & ROE

DATED:_____   _____

Attorneys for Debtor-in-Possession

FORM 26.2

Chapter 11 Plan

Attorneys for Debtor-in-Possession

UNITED STATES BANKRUPTCY COURT
District of Hoynes

In re	)	CASE NO.: 95-08888-Z11
	)	
JOHN SMITH CONTRACTING, INC.,	)	PLAN OF REORGANIZATION
	)	
Debtor-in-Possession.	)	
	)	

COMES NOW John Smith Contracting ,Inc., Debtor-in-Possession (hereinafter "John Smith") and hereby presents its Plan of Reorganization.

ARTICLE I

DEFINITIONS

As used in the Plan, the following terms shall have the respective meanings specified below, and such meanings shall be equally applicable to the singular and plural forms of the terms defined, unless the context otherwise requires:

1.1 <u>Abandoned Claim</u>. A claim is conclusively presumed to be abandoned whenever:

(A) The debtor has forwarded a payment under the Plan to the claimant at the address contained in the most recent master mailing list in the case or the address contained on the claimant's most recent proof of claim, if they are different, and the mail containing the Plan payment is returned as either "refused" or "non-deliverable";

(B) The debtor has made a payment under the Plan and the check issued to the claimant is not presented for payment within 60 days of the date that it was mailed to the claimant in the manner and to the addresses described in subsection 1.1(A) above, or;

(C)   The claimant expresses its intent to abandon its claim in whole or part.

1.2   _Administrative Claim_.   Any cost or expense of administration of this Chapter 11 case entitled to priority in accordance with the provisions of §§ 503(b), 506(c) and 507(a)(1) of the Bankruptcy Code, including, without limitation, any actual necessary expense of preserving the debtor's estate or of operating the debtor's business.

1.3   _Allowed Claim_.   Any claim (a) proof of which was timely and properly filed or which has been or hereafter is listed by John Smith in its schedules filed under §521(1) of the Bankruptcy Code as liquidated in amount and not disputed or contingent and, in either case, a claim to which (i) the claim is not an Undetermined Claim nor a Claim in an undetermined class, or (ii) any objection has been determined by a Final Order to the extent such objection has been determined in favor of a claimant, or (iii) an agreed amount has been determined by a stipulation or Final Order; (b) based on a Fee Application to the extent such Fee Application is approved by a Final Order; or (c) allowed under this Plan. Unless otherwise specified herein or by order of the Bankruptcy Court, "Allowed Claim" shall not include interest on such claim for the period from and after the petition date.

1.4   _Allowed Interest_.   The holder of an allowed interest, proof of which was timely and properly filed pursuant to Federal Rule of Bankruptcy Procedure 3002 and 3003 or which has been or hereafter is listed by a debtor on its list of equity security holders filed herein and not disputed or contingent, or which has been allowed under the Plan.

1.5 <u>Ballot Date</u>. The date set by the Bankruptcy Court as the last date for timely submission of a ballot accepting or rejecting the Plan.

1.6 <u>Bankruptcy Code</u>. The Bankruptcy Reform Act of 1978, as amended and as applicable to this Chapter 11 case, set forth in Title 11, United States Code.

1.7 <u>Bankruptcy Court</u>. The United States Bankruptcy Court for the District of Hoynes or such other court as may have jurisdiction over this Chapter 11 case or any relevant proceeding or matter, as applicable.

1.8 <u>Bankruptcy Rules</u>. The Federal Rules of Bankruptcy Procedure, as amended, applicable to cases pending before the Bankruptcy Court.

1.9 <u>Chapter 11 case</u>. The Chapter 11 case commenced by this Debtor-in-Possession.

1.10 <u>Claim</u>. Any right to payment from the Debtor-in-Possession that arose on or before the confirmation date whether or not such right is reduced to judgment, liquidated, filed contingent, matured, unmatured, disputed, undisputed, legal, equitable, secured or unsecured; or any right that arose on or before the consummation date to an equitable remedy for breach of performance if such breach gives rise to a right of payment from the debtor whether or not such right to an equitable remedy is reduced to judgment, fixed, contingent, matured, unmatured, disputed, undisputed, secured or unsecured. An entity with a claim is a claimant.

1.11 <u>Class</u>. Any one of Classes I through III, inclusive, as described in Article II of this Plan.

1.12 <u>Collateral</u>. Property in which John Smith has an interest that secures, in whole or in part, the payment of a claim.

1.13 <u>Confirmation Date</u>. The date of entry of the Confirmation Order in accordance with the provisions of the Bankruptcy Code; provided however, that if on motion the Confirmation Order or consummation of the Plan is stayed pending appeal, then the Confirmation date shall be the date of entry of the Final Order vacating such stay or the date on which such stay expires or is no longer in effect. The Confirmation date may also be referred to as the Effective Date of the Plan.

1.14 <u>Confirmation Order</u>. Order of the Bankruptcy Court Confirming the Plan and approving the transactions contemplated therein.

1.15 <u>Contested Claim</u>. Any claim as to which any party in interest has interposed an objection in accordance with the Bankruptcy Code and the Bankruptcy Rules, this Plan or orders of the Bankruptcy Court, which objection has not been withdrawn or determined by a Final Order; provided, however, that any Claim allowed under this Plan shall not be a Contested Claim.

1.16 <u>Creditor</u>. Any entity that is the holder of a Claim.

1.17 <u>Debtor-in-Possession</u>. John Smith as Debtor-in-

Possession in this Chapter 11 case commenced September 17, 1995.

1.18 <u>Disallowed Claim</u>. A Claim to the extent that such Claim was disallowed or deemed withdrawn by a Final Order or by written agreement of the holder thereof.

1.19 <u>Disclosure Statement</u>. The Disclosure Statement corresponding to this Plan as conditionally approved by the Bankruptcy Court pursuant to 11 U.S.C. §1125(f).

1.20 <u>Distribution</u>. Any payments provided for under the terms of and during the life of the Plan.

1.21 <u>Effective Date</u>. The date falling ninety (90) calendar days after entry of the Confirmation Order in accordance with the provisions of the Bankruptcy Code, or when surplus funds sufficient to fully satisfy all Unclassified and the Class I claims are on hand, whichever comes first; provided, however, that if on motion the Confirmation Order or consummation of the Plan is stayed pending appeal, then the Effective Date shall be that date falling thirty calendar days after entry of the Final Order vacating such stay or the date on which such stay expired or is no longer in effect. The Effective Date may also be referred to as the Consummation Date of the Plan.

1.22 <u>Equity Security Holder</u>. The holder of any Allowed Interest.

1.23 <u>Fee Applications</u>. Applications of Professional Persons under §§ 330 or 503 of the Bankruptcy Code for the allowance of compensation and reimbursement of expenses in the Chapter 11 case.

1.24 _Final Order_. An order or judgment which has not been reversed, stayed, modified or amended and (a) as to which (i) time to appeal or seek review or rehearing has expired and to which no appeal or petition for certiorari review or rehearing is pending, or (ii) appeal, review, reargument or certiorari of the order has been sought, and the order has been affirmed or the request for review, reargument or certiorari has been denied and the time to seek a further appeal, review, reargument or certiorari has expired; and (b) as a result of which such order shall become final and non-appealable in accordance with applicable law.

1.25 _Petition Date_. September 17, 1995.

1.26 _Plan_. This Plan of Reorganization proposed by John Smith either in its present form or as may be amended or modified from time to time.

1.27 _Post Confirmation Expenses_. All fees and expenses of Professional Persons and their employees incurred after the Confirmation Date.

1.28 _Priority Claim_. Any Claim, other than an Administrative Claim or a secured tax claim, to the extent entitled to priority of payment pursuant to 11 U.S.C. §507(a).

1.29 _Professional Person_. Persons retained or to be compensated pursuant to 11 U.S.C. §§ 326, 327, 328, 330, 503(b) and 1103.

1.30 _Pro Rata_. The proportion that the amount of the Claims against John Smith in a particular Class bears to the aggregate amount of all claims (including Undetermined Claims until allowed or disallowed) against John Smith in such Class.

1.31 _Secured Claim_. A Claim of a creditor arising on or before the Petition Date that is secured by a lien in property of John Smith or that is subject to setoff pursuant to 11 U.S.C. §553, to the extent of the value of such creditor's interest in the Debtor-in-Possession's interest in the property, or to the extent of the amount of the setoff, as applicable.

1.32 _Secured Creditor_. Any claimant that is the holder of a secured claim, to the extent of the value of the collateral securing such claim.

1.33 _Surplus Operating Revenue/Business Profits_. shall mean any accumulated cash held by the Debtor-in-Possession on the first day of any quarter in which payments must be made less operating capital in the amount of Six Thousand One Hundred Dollars ($6,100.00).

1.34 _Tax Claim_. Any claim of a governmental unit consisting of a tax claim that is either secured or entitled to priority of payment pursuant to 11 U.S.C. §507 (a)(8).

1.35 _Undetermined Claim or Interest_. A claim or interest, including, without limitation, (a) a Contested Claim or interest, (b) a claim arising from the rejection of executory contracts or unexpired leases pursuant to the Plan, (c) a Claim or Interest that is unliquidated or contingent, (d) a Claim as to which on or before the Confirmation Date the Debtor-in-Possession-in-Possession has not yet made a determination whether or not to object and (e) a Fee Claim that is not an allowed Claim or Disallowed Claim.

1.36 _Unsecured Claim_. An unsecured claim that is not (a)

entitled to priority pursuant to the Bankruptcy Code, or (b) subordinated for purposes of distribution to any unsecured claim pursuant to 11 U.S.C. § 510.

1.37 <u>Unsecured Creditor</u>. Any creditor that is the holder of an Unsecured Claim.

1.38 <u>Working (operating) Capital</u>. shall mean those funds that are necessary for the Debtor-in-Possession to conduct business on a daily basis in a sum never to exceed Six Thousand One Hundred Dollars ($6,100.00) per quarter.

1.39 <u>Other Definitions</u>. Whenever any word, words or phrase which are defined by any provision of the Bankruptcy Code are used herein, then, unless this Plan or the context specifically establish a different meaning, such word, words or phrase shall, for purposes of this Plan, have the same meaning as that established by the Bankruptcy Code.

II

<u>CLASSIFICATION OF CLAIMS AND EQUITY INTERESTS</u>

The Creditors and other holders of claims or interests of the Debtor-in-Possession-in-Possession are divided into the following classes:

A. <u>Unclassified Claims pursuant to 11 U.S.C.§1123(a)(1).</u>

<u>Administrative Claims</u>. This class includes the Claims of Professional Persons, and any other claims which are entitled to priority pursuant to 11 U.S.C. §507(a)(1), including the claims of Court approved Professional Persons retained by John Smith for services rendered and costs advanced in the present Chapter 11, estimated to be approximately Nine Thousand Five Hundred Dollars ($9,500.00) or more on the Confirmation date,

including any fees which may have been previously approved by the Court.

Priority Tax Claims. This class consists of unsecured Tax Claims of governmental units entitled to priority pursuant to 11 U.S.C. §507(a)(8), estimated to be $16,000.

B. Classified Claims pursuant to 11 U.S.C. §1123(a)(1).

2.1 Class I - Consists of the secured claims of Daniel, Inc. and Rafeal, Inc.

2.2 Class II - Consists of the general unsecured non-disputed and general unsecured disputed claims.

2.3 ClassIII - Consists of the claim of the equity security holder.

ARTICLE III

TREATMENT OF CLAIMS AND EQUITY INTERESTS

The Plan provides for the creation of three (3) classes of claims and interests and two groups of unclassified claims pursuant to 11 U.S.C. §1123(a)(1). The claims and interests shall be paid or satisfied in the following manner. All distributions under the Plan shall be free and clear of all liens, claims and encumbrances except as otherwise provided herein.

3.1 Administrative Claims. All administrative claims allowed by Order of the Bankruptcy Court, after hearing and approval of the amounts of the claims, shall be paid in full upon Court approval, unless otherwise agreed to by the Debtor-in-Possession-in-Possession and the holder of the claim. The source of payment to this claimant shall come from Debtor-in-Possession's business profits.

3.2 <u>Priority Tax Claims</u>. Priority Tax Claims shall be paid on a deferred cash payment basis, commencing on the Effective Date of the Plan and monthly thereafter for a period not exceeding six (6) years from the date of assessment, of a value, as of the Effective Date of the Plan, equal to the allowed amount of such claims. Such monthly payments shall include interest at the rate of ten percent (10%) per annum, and shall retain unaltered any liens that existed on the petition date to secure payment of the claims.

The earliest date of assessment of an IRS tax claim is September 21, 1994. The latest date of assessment of an IRS tax claim is December 20, 1995. Therefore, all tax claims must be fully satisfied through the Plan by December 20, 2001.

Payments to tax creditors are based upon an estimate of approximately Sixteen Thousand Dollars ($16,000.00) of pre-petition aggregate priority tax claims amortized on a monthly basis for six (6) years utilizing a 10% annual interest rate. These payments are estimated to be approximately Two Hundred Ninety Six Dollars ($296.00) per month for the life of the Plan. Please refer to the Disclosure Statement of even date herewith for further particulars concerning the priority tax claims.

3.3 <u>Class I</u> - Class I Claimants shall be paid in the following manner:

<u>Class I(a)</u> - Daniel, Inc. - This creditor, holding a security interest in Debtor-in-Possession's forklift, is owed a balance of approximately Eighteen Thousand Nine Hundred Twenty Six Dollars ($18,926.00). Monthly payments are One

Thousand Twenty Five Dollars ($1,025.00). Payments will continue to be made within the ordinary course of business, on the terms as originally agreed upon or as altered by the Court pursuant to ruling after a relief from stay motion. It is anticipated that this creditor will be paid in full fifteen (15) months after the Effective Date of the Plan.

Class I(b) - Rafeal, Inc. - This creditor, holding a security interest in Debtor-in-Possession's 1993 Chevrolet Truck, is currently owed a balance of approximately Thirteen Thousand Two Hundred Seventy Nine Dollars ($13,279.00). Monthly payments are Four Hundred Thirty Four Dollars ($434.00) per month. The agreement between Debtor-in-Possession and this creditor provides for designated monthly payments until June, 1998, at which time a balloon payment is due in the amount of Six Thousand Five Hundred Ninety Four Dollars ($6,594.00). Debtor-in-Possession intends to either pay the balloon payment out of working capital (see Definition of Working Capital - paragraph 1.38 within) or exercises its option to renew monthly payments for another year (June, 1999) at the end of which time the balloon payment would then be due in the amount of One Thousand Three Hundred Seventy Nine Dollars ($1,379.00)

3.4 Class II - The Class II Claimants will receive quarterly payments, in pari passu, from the Effective Date of the Plan until Plan completion. Payments will commence at the end of the first full calendar quarter after payment to the Administrative Claims. It is estimated that the total distribution to the Class II Claimants will be approximately

Two Hundred Eight Thousand Nine Hundred Forty Six Dollars($208,946.00), which will eventually allow Class II claimants to receive payment in full of their claims. Such distribution shall be in full satisfaction of such claims. Commencing on the Effective Date, or at the end of the first full calendar quarter falling after the Effective Date and after payment pursuant to the Plan to the Administrative claimants, the Class II claimants shall receive a pro rata distribution of all surplus funds. Thereafter, distributions to the Class II claimants shall be made at the end of every succeeding calendar quarter until all claims have been paid in full.

If the IRS priority tax claims are found to be substantially in excess of Sixteen Thousand Dollars ($16,000.00), the dividend to Class II claimants may be adversely impacted.

3.5 <u>Class III</u>. John Smith is the only equity security holder of the Debtor-in-Possession. The equity security holder shall take nothing under the Plan until completion of payments to all prior creditors at which time this Plan shall be deemed to be completed. Upon Plan completion, all rights will revest in the Debtor-in-Possession.

ARTICLE IV

EXECUTORY CONTRACTS

The Debtor-in-Possession will assume the unexpired lease on its business location. Should it be found that there exists any other executory contracts in connection with this proceeding, such executory contracts shall be deemed rejected by the Debtor-in-Possession for purposes of this Plan. Any claimant having a claim as a result of such rejection shall be deemed to have a Class II claim.

ARTICLE V

METHODS OF DISTRIBUTION

5.1 <u>Claims Resolution and Distribution</u>. On the Effective Date, the Debtor-in-Possession-in-Possession shall distribute all surplus funds to satisfy Unclassified and Allowed Claims as set forth in Article III, supra.

5.2 <u>Unclaimed Cash</u>. If any entity entitled to receive a distribution under the Plan cannot be located at the time such distribution is made, then such distribution shall be deemed an abandoned claim.

5.3 <u>Assumption of Liabilities</u>. As of the Effective Date, the liability for and obligation to make the distributions required under the Plan, including the payment of post-confirmation expenses, shall be vested in the Debtor-in-Possession-in-Possession as the Reorganized Debtor-in-Possession. ARTICLE VI

PROCEDURES REGARDING CONFIRMATION

6.1 <u>Conditional Approval of Disclosure Statement</u>. Following the filing of a Disclosure Statement as provided for by Bankruptcy Rule 3016(c), the Court shall hold a hearing on not less than 25 days notice to the Debtor-in-Possession, creditors, equity security holders and other parties in interest as provided for by Bankruptcy Rule 2002 to consider the Disclosure Statement and any objections or modifications thereto. Pursuant to 11 U.S.C. §1125(f), John Smith, as an electing small business, shall ask the court to conditionally approve the Disclosure Statement, permit the solicitation of acceptances or rejections to the Plan and set the final hearing on approval of the Disclosure Statement with the hearing on Confirmation of the Plan. The Plan and Disclosure Statement shall be mailed with the notice of the hearing only to the Debtor-in-Possession, any trustee or committee appointed under the Code, the Securities and Exchange Commission and any party in interest who requests in writing a copy of the Plan or Disclosure Statement. Objections to the Disclosure Statement shall be filed with the Court and served on the Debtor-in-Possession, the trustee, any committee appointed under the Code and such other entity as may be designated by the Court, at any time prior to conditional approval of the Disclosure Statement or by such other date as the Court may fix.

6.2 <u>Dates Fixed for Voting on Plan and Confirmation</u>. On or before conditional approval of the Disclosure Statement, the Court shall fix a time within which the holders of claims and interests may accept or reject the Plan and may fix a date for the hearing on final approval of the Disclosure Statement and confirmation of the Plan.

6.3 <u>Transmission and Notice to Creditors and Equity Security Holders</u>. On conditional approval of the Disclosure Statement, the Debtor-in-Possession-in-Possession, trustee, proponent of the Plan, or clerk as ordered by the Court shall mail to all creditors and equity security holders (1) the Plan, or a Court approved summary of the Plan; (2) the

Disclosure Statement conditionally approved by the Court; (3) notice of the time within which acceptances and rejections of such Plan may be filed; (4) notice of any date fixed for the hearing on confirmation; and (5) such other information as the Court may direct including any opinion of the Court approving the Disclosure Statement or a Court approved summary of the opinion. In addition, a form of ballot conforming to Official Form No. 30 shall be mailed to creditors and equity security holders entitled to vote on the Plan. In the event the opinion of the Court is not transmitted or only a summary of the Plan is transmitted, the opinion of the Court or the Plan shall be provided on request of a party in interest at the expense of the proponent of the Plan. For the purposes of this subdivision, creditors and equity security holders shall include holders of stocks, bonds, debentures, notes and other securities of record at the date the order conditionally approving the Disclosure Statement was entered.

ARTICLE VII

POST-CONFIRMATION ASPECTS

7.1 <u>Role of the Creditors Committee</u>. On the Effective Date, any creditors committee appointed in this case shall cease to exist with respect to the reorganized Debtor-in-Possession.

7.2 <u>Role of the Debtor-in-Possession-in-Possession</u>. On and after the Effective Date, title to all property of John Smith, real or personal, as well as rights to commence future litigation, shall be vested in John Smith as a reorganized Debtor-in-Possession consistent with the provisions of this

Plan.

7.3 _Verification Procedure_. During the life of the Plan, in the event that John Smith is required to make payments to any class of claimants over a period of time, John Smith will be required to provide a quarterly report to all creditors and parties in interest entitled to such payments regarding the progress of the Plan.

7.4 _Resolution of Disputes and Undetermined Claims or Interests_. Disputes regarding the proper classification of Claims not otherwise specifically classified shall be resolved pursuant to procedures established by the Bankruptcy Code, the Bankruptcy Rules, and other applicable law, the Bankruptcy Court and this Plan, and such resolution shall not be a condition precedent to confirmation or consummation of this Plan.

7.5 _Post-Confirmation Management_. John Smith, individually, President of the Debtor-in-Possession, currently grosses Sixty One Thousand Nine Hundred Twenty Dollars ($61,920.00) per annum as manager of the Debtor-in-Possession.

ARTICLE VIII

PROVISIONS FOR RETENTION OF JURISDICTION BY THE

BANKRUPTCY COURT FOR SUPERVISION OF THE PLAN

8.1 _Scope of Jurisdiction_. The Bankruptcy Court shall retain jurisdiction over the Chapter 11 case for the following purposes:

(a) determining any and all objections to the allowance of classifications or subordinations of Claims or Interests, including all counterclaims, cross-claims or third party complaints arising therefrom (whether expressed by way of a contested matter or adversary proceeding);

(b) determining any and all fee applications and any other fees and expenses authorized to be paid or reimbursed under the Bankruptcy Code;

(c) determining any and all pending applications for the rejection or assumption of executory contracts or for any leases to which the Debtor-in-Possession is a party or with respect to which it may be liable, to set bar dates arising from the rejection of any of the same, and to hear and determine,; and if need be, to liquidate any and all claims arising therefrom;

(d) determining any and all applications, adversary proceedings, and contested or litigated matters before the Bankruptcy Court and commenced before the expiration of six months after the Consummation Date;

(e) modifying the Plan or remedying any defect or omission or reconciling any inconsistency in any order of the Bankruptcy Court including the Confirmation Order to the extent authorized by the Bankruptcy Code;

(f) determining all controversies, suits and disputes that may arise in connection with the interpretation, enforcement or consummation of this Plan;

(g) implementing the Plan, including without limitation, entering appropriate orders to protect the Debtor-in-Possession from creditor actions;

(h) entering a final decree closing the Chapter 11 case;

and

(j) determining such other matters as may arise in connection with this Plan or the Confirmation Order.

8.2 <u>Failure of the Bankruptcy Court to Exercise Jurisdiction</u>. If the Bankruptcy Court abstains from exercising, or declines to exercise jurisdiction or is otherwise without jurisdiction over any matter arising out of the Chapter 11 case, including the matters set forth in this Article, this Article shall have no effect upon and shall not control, prohibit or limit the exercise of jurisdiction by any other Court having competent jurisdiction with respect to such matter.

ARTICLE IX

IMPAIRED AND UNIMPAIRED CLASSES

AND VOTING ON THE PLAN

9.1 To be confirmed, the Plan must be approved by more than fifty percent (50%) in number and sixty-six and two-thirds percent (66.67%) in dollar amount of votes actually cast by each impaired class in Classes I-II. Two-thirds in percentage of interest must approve the Plan for Class III to accept the Plan. "Impaired Class" is generally defined by the Bankruptcy Code as those classes of claimants whose legal, equitable or contractual rights are altered under the terms of the Plan.

In determining whether the Plan has been accepted by each class, votes will only be counted if submitted by a creditor whose claim is duly scheduled by the Debtor-in-Possession as undisputed, noncontingent and unliquidated, or , who has filed with the Court a proof of Claim on or before the Claims Bar Date set in this case, which has not been disallowed or suspended prior to the computation of the votes on the Plan. The Ballot form which you will receive does not constitute a proof of claim. If you are uncertain whether or not your claim has been correctly scheduled, you should check the Debtor-in-Possession's schedules which are on file in the Bankruptcy Court. The Bankruptcy Court will not provide this information over the telephone.

9.2 Unimpaired Classes. Class I is unimpaired under the Plan as defined by §1124 of the Bankruptcy Code. By virtue of its status as an "unimpaired" class of claims under the Bankruptcy Code, this class is deemed to have accepted the Plan in accordance with Bankruptcy Code §1126(f). Accordingly, the Debtor-in-Possession-in-Possession is not required to solicit votes of such Class with respect to the acceptance or rejection of the Plan.

9.3 Impaired Voting Classes. The Claims of claimants or interest holders in classes II-III are impaired by this Plan. Such claimants or interest holders shall be entitled to vote to accept or reject the Plan. A Class of claims shall have accepted the Plan if the Plan is accepted by the holders of at least two-thirds in dollar amount and more than one-half in number of the claims of each such class that vote and whose vote is received by the date fixed by the Court.

9.4 Reservation of §1129(b) Rights. Upon any rejections of the Plan by Classes II or III, John Smith shall request that the Bankruptcy Court confirm the Plan in accordance with

§1129(b) of the Bankruptcy Code.

Under 11 U.S.C. §1129(b)(1), a plan proponent may effectuate a cramdown, confirmation of the plan over rejection by a dissenting class of claims or interests, if the Court finds that the Plan is fair and equitable and does not unfairly discriminate as to a class of claims or interests.

A plan is fair and equitable as to a class of secured claims pursuant to 11 U.S.C. §1129(b)(2)(A) if a class of secured claims retains its liens and is either paid in full over the life of the plan, paid in full from the proceeds of a sale of any property subject to the secured claim, or if the holder of a secured claim receives the indubitable value of its claim. In the present Plan, it is John Smith's contention that this test is met with respect to the secured claims in Class I.

A plan is fair and equitable with respect to a class of unsecured claims pursuant to 11 U.S.C. §1129(b)(2)(B) if the class of claims is paid in full over the life of the plan or if no junior class of claims or interests receives a dividend under the Plan. In the present Plan, it will be John Smith's contention that since all classes of claims are being paid in full that the Plan is fair and equitable with respect to all senior classes.

A plan is fair and equitable with respect to a class of interests pursuant to 11 U.S.C. §1129(b)(2)(C) if all interest holders within the class retain their interests and if no junior class receives a dividend. In the present Plan, it will be John Smith's contention, in addition to those set forth above, that the interest holders will retain no interests in John Smith inconsistent with the provisions of the Plan and consistent with the rights of all senior classes provided for under the Plan.

ARTICLE X

CONDITIONS PRECEDENT TO CONSUMMATION

10.1 The following shall be the condition precedent to consummation of the Plan:

(a) The Confirmation Order shall have become a Final Order of the Bankruptcy Court.

ARTICLE XI

DISCHARGE, SURRENDER AND CANCELLATION

OF CLAIMS AND INTERESTS

11.1 <u>Discharge of Claims</u>. Except as otherwise provided herein or in the Confirmation Order, the rights afforded in this Plan and the payments and distributions to be made hereunder shall be in complete exchange for, and in full satisfaction, discharge and release of all existing debts and claims of any kind, nature or description whatsoever against the Debtor-in-Possession-in-Possession, or of its assets or properties; and upon the Effective Date, all existing claims against the Debtor-in-Possession-in-Possession shall be, and be deemed to be exchanged, satisfied, discharged and released in full and all holders of claims shall be precluded from asserting against the Debtor-in-Possession-in-Possession or its assets or properties any other or further claim based upon any act or omission, transaction or other activity of any kind or nature that occurred prior to the Effective Date, whether or not such holder filed a proof of claim.

11.2 _Effect of Confirmation Order_. Except as provided for in this Plan, the Confirmation order shall be a judicial determination of discharge of John Smith from all debts that arose before the Effective Date and any liability on a claim that is determined under Bankruptcy Code §502 as if such claim had arisen before the Effective Date, whether or not a proof of claim based on any such debt or liability is filed under Bankruptcy Code §501 and whether or not a claim based on such debt or liability is allowed under Bankruptcy Code §502, and operates as an injunction against the commencement or continuation of an action, the employment of process of an act, to collect, recover or offset any such debt as the liability of the Debtor-in-Possession-in-Possession, whether or not discharge of such debt is waived.

11.3 _Surrender of Instruments and Release of Liens_. Except as otherwise provided in the Plan, each holder of an instrument evidencing a Claim shall surrender such instrument to the Debtor-in-Possession-in-Possession and the Debtor-in-Possession-in-Possession shall distribute to the holder thereof the distributions provided for in the Plan. No distribution under the Plan shall be made to or on behalf of any such holder of such a claim unless and until such instrument is received or the non-availability of such instrument is established to the reasonable satisfaction of the Debtor-in-Possession-in-Possession. Each Claimant who is to receive a distribution under the Plan in complete satisfaction of a Secured Claim shall not receive such distributions until such claimant executes a release of such lien in recordable form and delivers the same to the Debtor-in-Possession-in-Possession. Any such holder who fails to surrender such instrument or satisfactorily explain its non-availability or to execute such release of liens within one year of the Effective Date shall be deemed to have no further Claim and shall not participate in any distribution under this Plan.

11.4 <u>Post-Confirmation Effect of Evidence of Claim</u>. Notes and other evidences of Claims' shall, upon the Effective Date, represent only the right to participate in the distributions contemplated by this Plan or matters reserved by the Plan.

ARTICLE XII

MISCELLANEOUS

12.1 <u>Means for Execution of the Plan</u>. All payments to be made under this Plan shall come from the profits to be generated out of the future operations of the Debtor-in-Possession's current business. Payments from these profits will be used to pay approved Claimants in all Classes. The Debtor-in-Possession expects to generate Fifty Five Thousand Two Hundred Dollars ($55,200.00) in profits annually for the next approximately five (5) years to be distributed as Plan dividends. These profits are evidenced by Debtor-in-Possession's pro-forma which is attached hereto as Exhibit "A" to the accompanying Disclosure Statement. The pro-forma was prepared by John Smith, Debtor-in-Possession's President.

12.2 <u>Amendment</u>. The Plan may be altered, amended or

modified by the Debtor-in-Possession-in-Possession before or after the Confirmation Date in the manner provided for by 11 U.S.C. §1127. A holder of a Claim or Interest that has accepted or rejected the Plan shall be deemed to have accepted or rejected, as the case may be, the Plan as modified, unless, within the time fixed by the Bankruptcy Court, such holder changes its previous acceptance or rejection.

12.3 <u>Headings</u>. The headings used in the Plan are inserted for convenience only and neither constitute a portion of the Plan nor, in any manner, affect the provisions or interpretations of the Plan.

12.4 <u>Severability</u>. Should any provision in the Plan be determined to be unenforceable, such determination shall in no way limit or affect the enforceability and operative effect of any other provision(s) of the Plan.

12.5 <u>Successors and Assigns</u>. The rights and obligations of any person named or referred to in the Plan shall be binding upon, and shall inure to the benefit of, the successors and assigns of such person.

12.6 <u>Internal References</u>. The words "herein", "hereof", "hereto", "hereunder" and other words of similar import refer to the Plan as a whole and not to any particular section, subsection or clause contained in the Plan.

12.7 <u>Current Book Accounts</u>. To the extent the Debtor-in-Possession has maintained current book accounts with suppliers post-petition, such accounts shall be reaffirmed herein and shall be paid according to the terms and conditions thereof in the ordinary course of future operation.

12.8 <u>Retention of Assets</u>. On the Date of Confirmation, the Debtor-in-Possession shall be fully restored to the assets of the estate subject to the terms and conditions of this Plan.

12.9 <u>Acceleration of the Plan</u>. To the extent that the Debtor-in-Possession finds it desirable to accelerate performance of the Plan, the Debtor-in-Possession may do so without further approval of the Court.

12.10 <u>Notices</u>. All notices any payments required or permitted to be made in accordance with the Plan shall be in writing and shall be made by placing the notice or payment in the United States Mail with first-class postage affixed and addressed to the holder of an allowed claim at their last known address. It shall be the duty of such claimants to inform the Debtor-in-Possession of any changes in address. Failure to do so prior to completion of the Plan shall be deemed a waiver of any amounts left due and owing to such creditors.

DOE & ROE

DATED:_____   By:_____

FORM 26.3

Chapter 11 Disclosure Statement

Attorneys for

UNITED STATES BANKRUPTCY COURT
Southern District of California

In re	) CASE NO.: 95-08888-Z11
	)
JOHN SMITH CONTRACTING, INC.,	) DISCLOSURE STATEMENT
	)
Debtor.	)
	)
_____	)

On or about February 17, 1995, John Smith Contracting, Inc., herein referred to as "John Smith" or "Debtor", filed a Petition for Relief under Chapter 11, Title 11, United States Bankruptcy Code. Concurrent herewith, Smith has filed a Plan or Reorganization hereinafter known as the "Plan". Pursuant to 11 U.S.C. § 1125 of the Bankruptcy Code, Smith has prepared and filed this Disclosure Statement, along with the Plan, for the Court's approval and submission to the holders of claims and interests with respect to Smith's assets and liabilities.

The purpose of this Disclosure Statement is to provide the holders of claims against Smith adequate and reasonable information about the financial affairs of John Smith. Along with this Disclosure Statement, the Plan is attached to further assist all claimants to make and informed judgment regarding the merits of approving the Plan.

NO REPRESENTATION CONCERNING JOHN SMITH (PARTICULARLY AS TO THE VALUE OF PROPERTY) ARE AUTHORIZED BY JOHN SMITH, OTHER THAN AS SET FORTH IN THIS STATEMENT. ANY REPRESENTATIONS OR INDUCEMENTS

MADE TO SECURE YOUR ACCEPTANCE WHICH ARE OTHER THAN AS CONTAINED IN THIS STATEMENT SHOULD NOT BE RELIEF UPON IN ARRIVING AT A DECISION AND SUCH ADDITIONAL REPRESENTATIONS AND INDUCEMENTS SHOULD BE REPORTED TO COUNSEL FOR JOHN SMITH WHO IN TURN SHALL DELIVER SUCH INFORMATION TO THE BANKRUPTCY COURT FOR SUCH ACTION AS MAY BEEN DEEMED APPROPRIATE.

THE INFORMATION CONTAINED HEREIN HAS NOT BEEN SUBJECT TO A CERTIFIED AUDIT. FOR THE FOREGOING REASON, JOHN SMITH IS UNABLE TO WARRANT OR REPRESENT THAT THE INFORMATION CONTAINED HEREIN IS WITHOUT ANY INACCURACIES; ALTHOUGH GREAT EFFORT HAS BEEN MADE TO BE ACCURATE.

I

INTRODUCTION

John Smith, incorporated in early 1993, is a general contracting business, specializing in sub-contracting commercial framing.

The business grew much more rapidly than anticipated. Unfortunately, John Smith did not possess sufficient manpower to adequately supervise the jobs that it took on concurrent with this rapid growth. As a consequence of this lack of supervision, many jobs lost money instead of generating a profit. The loss of revenue resulted in John Smith's inability to keep current with its payroll tax obligations and worker's compensation insurance premiums. One week prior to the filing, the Internal Revenue Service levied upon John Smith's bank accounts and seized approximately Ninety Seven Thousand Dollars ($97,000.00). The seizure forced John Smith to seek protection by filing this Chapter 11 proceeding.

Since the time of the filing, John Smith has attempted to restructure itself to eliminate the problems that precipitated its financial difficulties. This restructuring includes the following changes:

1. Reduction in support employees from twenty five (25) to fifteen (15);

2. Reduction in administrative staff;

3. More selectivity in job bidding by concentrating on a minimum of jobs that will evidence the maximum profit;

5. Specializing in a specific area of construction, i.e., commercial construction of supermarkets and research and development building;

6. Elimination of employee benefit programs for all support employees (if the employee wants the program, he must pay for it himself);

7. Adoption of conservation approach to business expenditures; and

8. Limitation of employee use of company vehicles.

These changes have resulted in a significant profit in recent months which has enabled the Debtor to pay all accrued administrative expenses in full.

John Smith is the President of the Debtor and its sole shareholder. Mr. John Smith's responsibilities include overseeing the entire operations of the business. More specifically, these duties entail the following:

1. Supervision of all proposals for new projects;

2. Soliciting new clients for future projects;

3. Meetings with contractors and developers for new and existing projects;

4. Supervision of all financial transactions;

5. Determination of company guidelines and policies;

6. Review and execution of all legal contracts, change orders and legal tax forms; and

7. Meetings with legal counsel whenever necessary.

Mr. John Smith spends a total of approximately 55 hours per week in performance of his duties and responsibilities. His gross monthly salary, which has been approved by this Court, is Five Thousand One Hundred Sixty Dollars ($5,160.00). Mr. John Smith has been active in the contracting business since 1984.

SUMMARY OF BACKLOG & WORK IN PROGRESS

Work In Progress	Contract Amount	% of Completion	Completion Date
Airport Terminal Remodeling	$327,307.00	85	3/7/97
Skylar Shopping Center	$ 64,247.00	5	4/3/97
Dana Austin Civic	$113,000.00	3	4/29/97

Work Backlog	Contract Amount	Commencement Date
Happy Kids Day Care Center	$134,824.00	12/15/96
Morris Schulman Building	$175,373.00	1/15/96
Julie Rasmussen's Toll House Cookie Restaurant	$152,533.00	11/15/96

II

SUMMARY OF CLAIMS AND PLAN

The Plan provides for the creation of three (3) classes of claims and interests and two groups of unclassified claims pursuant

238

to 11 U.S.C. §1123(a)(1). The claims and interests shall be paid or satisfied in the following manner. All distributions under the Plan shall be free and clear of all liens, claims and encumbrances except as otherwise provided herein.

The Plan is an operating plan in that John Smith will distribute the proceeds to classes of claims in the order of priority mandated by the Bankruptcy Code from surplus operating revenues generated from a continuation of the business.

Essentially, administrative clailms will be paid from funds on hand on the Effective Date. To the extent that funds are available, other classes will receive dividends on the Effective Date. Thereafter, distributions will be made on a pro rata basis each quarter to each class entitled thereto, until all classes have. been paid in full.

Unclassified Claims pursuant to 11 U.S.C.§1123(a)(1).

2.1 Administrative Claims. Claims pursuant to §503 of the Unnited States Bankruptcy Code are expected to be incurred and payable by John Smith. These expenses include attorney fees of Doe & Roe in an amount estimated to be Nine Thousand Five Hundred Dollars ($9,500.00). This estimate is based upon the premise that the current Plan is confirmed and with the understanding that counsel's fees are subject to approval of the United States Bankruptcy Court.

2.2 All Other Administrative Expenses. These are claims currently being incurred and paid by John Smith in the normal course of business which do not require approval of the Bankruptcy Court to be paid pursuant to 11 U.S.C. §364(a).

2.3 <u>Priority Tax Claims</u>. This class consists of priority claims pursuant to 11 U.S.C. §507(a)(8) filed by the Internal Revenue Service ("IRS"). This IRS has filed claims of One Hundred Thirteen Thousand Dollars ($113,000.00). John Smith disputes the amount of this claim and believes that the correct amount is approximately Sixteen Thousand Dollars ($16,000) representing payroll tax liabilities for the third quarter of 1995. John Smith believes that the IRS claim has not properly credited the pre-petition seizures made in August, 1995 and has not credited payments made for the month of September, 1995.

The Debtor will endeavor to reconcile the IRS claim prior to the confirmation hearing in this proceeding. If the IRS claim is found to substantially exceed Sixteen Thousand Dollars ($16,000.00), the Plan's feasibility will be adversely impacted.

<u>Classified Claims pursuant to 11 U.S.C. §1123(a)(1)</u>.

2.4 <u>Class I: Secured Claims</u>. This class consists of the secured claims of the following entities:

<u>Class I (a)</u> - Daniel, Inc., in the current amount of Eighteen Thousand Nine Hundred Twenty Six Dollars ($18,926.00). Daniel, Inc., holds a security interest in a Lull 622 Forklift.

<u>Class I (b)</u> - Rafeal, Inc., in the current amount of Thirteen Thousand Two Hundred Seventy Nine Dollars ($13,279.00). Rafeal, Inc., holds a security interest in a 1993 Chevrolet.

2.5 <u>Class II: General Unsecured Claims</u>. This class consists of the general unsecured non-disputed creditors holding claims in the approximate total amount of Two Hundred Eight Thousand Nine Hundred Forty Six Dollars Twenty Five Cents ($208,946.25). This class also consists of general unsecured disputed claims of Jason

Flam and Sandler Cement in the aggregate amount of Seventy Three Thousand One Hundred Sixty Eight Dollars Thirty One Cents ($73,168.31).

2.6 <u>ClassIII: Equity Security Holder.</u> This class consists of the claim of John Smith, who is the only shareholder of the Debtor.

ARTICLE III

PLAN OF REORGANIZATION

The claims and interests shall be paid or satisfied in the following manner. All distributions under the Plan shall be free and clear of all liens, claims and encumbrances except as otherwise provided herein.

3.1 <u>Administrative Claims.</u> All administrative claims allowed by Order of the Bankruptcy Court, after hearing and approval of the amounts of the claims, shall be paid in full upon Court approval, unless otherwise agreed to by the Debtor-in-Possession-in-Possession and the holder of the claim. The source of payment to this claimant shall come from Debtor-in-Possession's Surplus Operating Revenues.

3.2 <u>Priority Tax Claims.</u> Priority Tax Claims shall be paid on a deferred cash payment basis, commencing on the Effective Date of the Plan and monthly thereafter for a period not exceeding six (6) years from the date of assessment, of a value, as of the Effective Date of the Plan, equal to the allowed amount of such claims. Such monthly payments shall include interest at the rate of ten percent (10%) per annum, and shall retain unaltered any liens that existed on the petition date to secure payment of the claims.

The earliest date of assessment of an IRS tax claim is September 21, 1994. The latest date of assessment of an IRS tax claim is December 20, 1995. Therefore, all tax claims must be fully satisfied through the Plan by December 20, 2001.

Payments to tax creditors are based upon an estimate of approximately Sixteen Thousand Dollars ($16,000.00) of pre-petition aggregate priority tax claims amortized on a monthly basis for six (6) years utilizing a 10% annual interest rate. These payments are estimated to be approximately Two Hundred Ninety Six Dollars ($296.00) per month for the life of the Plan.

3.3 Class I - Class I Claimants shall be paid in the following manner:

Class I(a) - Daniel, Inc. - This creditor, holding a security interest in Debtor-in-Possession's forklift, is owed a balance of approximately Eighteen Thousand Nine Hundred Twenty Six Dollars ($18,926.00). Monthly payments are One Thousand Twenty Five Dollars ($1,025.00). Payments will continue to be made within the ordinary course of business, on the terms as originally agreed upon or as altered by the Court pursuant to ruling after a relief from stay motion. It is anticipated that this creditor will be paid in full fifteen (15) months after the Effective Date of the Plan.

Class I(b) - Rafeal, Inc. - This creditor, holding a security interest in Debtor-in-Possession's 1993 Chevrolet Truck, is currently owed a balance of approximately Thirteen Thousand Two Hundred Seventy Nine Dollars ($13,279.00). Monthly payments are Four Hundred Thirty Four Dollars ($434.00) per month. The agreement between Debtor-in-Possession and this creditor provides for designated monthly payments until June, 1998, at which time a balloon payment is due in the amount of Six Thousand Five Hundred Ninety Four Dollars ($6,594.00). Debtor-in-Possession intends to either pay the balloon payment out of working capital or exercise its option to renew monthly payments for another year (June, 1999) at the end of which time the balloon payment would then be due in the amount of One Thousand Three Hundred Seventy Nine Dollars ($1,379.00)

3.4 <u>Class II</u> - The Class II Claimants will receive quarterly payments, in pari passu, from the Effective Date of the Plan until Plan completion. Payments will commence at the end of the first full calendar quarter after payment to the Administrative Claims. It is estimated that the total distribution to the Class II Claimants will be approximately Two Hundred Eight Thousand Nine Hundred Forty Six Dollars($208,946.00), which will eventually allow Class II claimants to receive payment in full of their claims. Such distribution shall be in full satisfaction of such claims. Commencing on the Effective Date, or at the end of the first full calendar quarter falling after the Effective Date and after payment pursuant to the Plan to the Administrative claimants, the Class II claimants shall receive a pro rata distribution of all surplus funds. Thereafter, distributions to the Class II claimants shall be made at the end of every succeeding calendar quarter until all claims have been paid in full.

The disputed claimholders of this class are Jason Flam and Sandler Cement. Jason Flam has alleged a claim for Fourteen Thousand One Hundred Seventy Seven Dollars Twenty Seven Cents ($14,177.27), and Sandler Cement has alleged a claim for Fifty Eight Thousand Nine Hundred Ninety One Dollars Four Cents ($58,991.04). It is John Smith's intention to object to these claims. Distributions otherwise payable to these disputed claims (as if they were allowed claimholders) shall be sequestered pending the outcome of the claims objections. In the event that a particular claim is disallowed, then any sequestered funds that would have been distributed as a dividend if the claim had been allowed, shall be distributed in pari passu to the remaining Class II Claimants.

As to the Flam claim, John Smith will assert that Flam has failed to credit payments made and services rendered in satisfaction of the claim. Sandler Cement delivered defective concrete on the Airport Remodeling job which has resulted in completion delays and the incurring of additional costs occasioned by having to replace Sandler Cement with Nach Concrete.

If the IRS priority tax claims are found to be substantially in excess of Sixteen Thousand Dollars ($16,000.00), the dividend to Class II claimants may be adversely impacted.

3.5 **Class III**. John Smith is the only equity security holder of the Debtor-in-Possession. The equity security holder shall take nothing under the Plan until completion of payments to all prior creditors at which time this Plan shall be deemed to be completed. Upon Plan completion, all rights will revest in the Debtor-in-Possession.

IV

EXECUTORY CONTRACTS

ARTICLE IV

EXECUTORY CONTRACTS

The Debtor-in-Possession will assume the unexpired lease on its business location. Should it be found that there exists any other executory contracts in connection with this proceeding, such executory contracts shall be deemed rejected by the Debtor-in-Possession for purposes of this Plan. Any claimant having a claim as a result of such rejection shall be deemed to have a Class II claim.

V

MISCELLANEOUS

5.1 Means for Execution of the Plan. All payments to be made under this Plan shall come from the profits to be generated out of the future operations of the Debtor's current business. Payments from these profits will be used to pay approved Claimants in all Classes. The Debtor expects to generate Fifty Five Thousand Two Hundred Dollars ($55,200.00) in profits annually for the next approximately five (5) years to be distributed as Plan dividends. These profits are evidenced by Debtor's pro-forma which is attached hereto as Exhibit "A" and incorporated herein by reference. The pro-forma was prepared by John Smith, Debtor's President.

5.2 Compensation. John Smith, President of the Debtor, currently grosses Sixty One Thousand Nine Hundred Twenty Dollars ($61,920.00) per annum as manager of the Debtor.

5.3 _Shareholder Information_. When the Debtor was incorporated, Twenty Thousand (20,000) shares were authorized at par value of Fifty Eight Dollars Fifty Six Cents ($58.56) per share. Two Thousand (2,000) shares have been issued. The Debtor's only shareholder is John Smith.

5.4 _Retention of Assets_. On the Date of Confirmation, the Debtor-in-Possession shall be fully restored to the assets of the estate subject to the terms and conditions of this Plan.

5.5 _Acceleration of the Plan_. To the extent that the Debtor-in-Possession finds it desirable to accelerate performance of the Plan, the Debtor-in-Possession may do so without further approval of the Court.

5.6 _Tax Consequences_. John Smith does not anticipate any adverse tax consequences to the estate inasmuch as the corporation is qualified under Subchapter S of the Internal Revenue Code, 26 U.S.C. §1361 et seq. Under Subchapter S, any income or losses are attributed to the shareholder on a pro rata basis.

5.7 _Claims Resolution and Distribution_. On the Effective Date, the Debtor-in-Possession-in-Possession shall distribute all surplus funds to satisfy Unclassified and Allowed Claims as set forth in Article III of the Plan.

5.8 _Unclaimed Cash_. If any entity entitled to receive a distribution under the Plan cannot be located at the time such distribution is made, then such distribution shall be deemed an abandoned claim.

5.9 _Assumption of Liabilities_. As of the Effective Date, the liability for and obligation to make the distributions required under the Plan, including the payment of post-confirmation expenses, shall be vested in the Debtor-in-Possession-in-Possession as the Reorganized Debtor-in-Possession.

5.10 <u>Additional Sources of Information</u>. Additional sources of information available to all creditors are the variuos schedules and reports filed John Smith in accordance with the provisions of the Bankruptcy Code and prior orders of the Court summarized below:

a. The "Chapter 11 Statement of Affairs for Debtor Engaged in Business; Schedules; and Statement of Executory Contracts" on file with the Bankruptcy Court; and

b. John Smith's monthly operating reports.

The Schedules and operating reports described above are available for inspection and review by the public in the Office of the Clerk of the United States Bankruptcy Court for the District of Hoynes, 325 West "F" Street, Carroll, Hoynes, 92101, during regular business hours (M-F 8:30 a.m. to 4:00 p.m.).

ARTICLE VI

PROCEDURES REGARDING CONFIRMATION

6.1 <u>Conditional Approval of Disclosure Statement</u>. Following the filing of a Disclosure Statement as provided for by Bankruptcy Rule 3016(c), the Court shall hold a hearing on not less than 25 days notice to the Debtor-in-Possession, creditors, equity security holders and other parties in interest as provided for by Bankruptcy Rule 2002 to consider the Disclosure Statement and any objections or modifications thereto. Pursuant to 11 U.S.C. §1125(f), John Smith, as an electing small business, shall ask the court to conditionally approve the Disclosure Statement, permit the solicitation of acceptances or rejections to the Plan and set the final hearing on approval of the Disclosure Statement with the hearing on Confirmation of the Plan. The Plan and Disclosure Statement shall be mailed with the notice of the hearing only to the Debtor-in-Possession, any trustee or committee appointed under the Code, the Securities and Exchange Commission and any party in interest who requests in writing a copy of the Plan or Disclosure Statement. Objections to the Disclosure Statement shall be filed with the Court and served on the Debtor-in-Possession, the trustee, any committee appointed under the Code and such other entity as may be designated by the Court, at any time prior to conditional approval of the Disclosure Statement or by such other date as the Court may fix.

6.2 <u>Dates Fixed for Voting on Plan and Confirmation</u>. On or before conditional approval of the Disclosure Statement, the Court shall fix a time within which the holders of claims and interests may accept or reject the Plan and may fix a date for the hearing on final approval of the Disclosure Statement and confirmation of the Plan.

6.3 <u>Transmission and Notice to Creditors and Equity Security Holders</u>. On conditional approval of the Disclosure Statement, the Debtor-in-Possession-in-Possession, trustee, proponent of the Plan, or clerk as ordered by the Court shall mail to all creditors and equity security holders (1) the Plan, or a Court approved summary of the Plan; (2) the Disclosure Statement conditionally approved by the Court; (3) notice of the time within which acceptances and rejections of such Plan may be filed; (4) notice of any date fixed for the hearing on confirmation; and (5) such other information as the Court may direct including any opinion of the Court approving the Disclosure Statement or a Court approved summary of the opinion. In addition, a form of ballot conforming to Official Form No. 30 shall be mailed to creditors and equity security holders entitled to vote on the Plan. In the event the opinion of the Court is not transmitted or only a summary of the Plan is transmitted, the opinion of the Court or the Plan shall be provided on request of a party in interest at the expense of the proponent of the Plan. For the purposes of this subdivision, creditors and equity security holders shall include holders of stocks, bonds, debentures, notes and other securities of record at the date the order conditionally approving the Disclosure Statement was entered.

6.4 <u>Hearing on Confirmation of the Plan</u>. The Bankruptcy Court will set a hearing date to determine whether the Plan has been accepted by the requisite number of claimants and classes of claimants, and whether the other requirements for confirmation of the Plan have been satisfied. Each creditor and interest holder will receive the Court's Notice of Hearing on Confirmation of the Plan, along with a ballot to be used in voting on the Plan.

VII

<u>LIQUIDATION ANALYSIS</u>

To obtain confirmation, John Smith must, among other things, demonstrate that each class of claims is receiving at least as much as it would receive if the estate were liquidated under Chapter 7 as of the Effective Date. This test, commonly known as the "best interests of creditors test", as provided for by 11 U.S.C. §1129(a)(7).

249

7.1 ASSETS AND LIABILITIES

John Smith expects that it will generate profits of Fifty Five Thousand Two Hundred Dollars ($55,200.00) per year for Plan distribution, or a total of Two Hundred Seventy Six Thousand Dollars ($276,000.00) during the five (5) year life of the Plan. Such revenues will be used to satisfy the different Classes of Claimants noted with this Plan.

These figures are as follows:

Adminnistrative	$ 9,500.00
Priority Tax	$ 16,000.00[1]
Class I	$ 32,209.00
Class II	$ 208,946.25[2]
Class III	-0-
TOTAL LIABILITIES	**$ 266,655.25**
Business Profits generated over a 60 month period	$ 276,000.00
TOTAL ASSETS	**$ 276,000.00**

7.2 Should liquidation become necessary, all creditors will receive less than what the Plan of Reorganization provides for as payment of their claims. This fact is based upon an updated summary of assets, which appraises the value of all the assets of the Debtor at One Hundred Ninety Six Thousand Two Hundred Sixty

---

[1] The IRS asserts a claim of $113,000.00 which John Smith disputes.

[2] This amount does not include the disputed claims of Jason Flam and Sandler Cement in the aggregate amount of $73,168.31.

Four Dollars and Thirty Five Cents ($196,264.35). This report, prepared by John Smith for the purpose of this Disclosure Statement, is attached hereto as Exhibit "B" and incorporated herein by reference.

ARTICLE VIII

POST-CONFIRMATION ASPECTS

8.1 <u>Role of the Creditors Committee</u>. On the Effective Date, any creditors committee appointed in this case shall cease to exist with respect to the reorganized Debtor-in-Possession.

8.2 <u>Role of the Debtor-in-Possession-in-Possession</u>. On and after the Effective Date, title to all property of John Smith, real or personal, as well as rights to commence future litigation, shall be vested in John Smith as a reorganized Debtor-in-Possession consistent with the provisions of this Plan.

8.3 <u>Verification Procedure</u>. During the life of the Plan, in the event that John Smith is required to make payments to any class of claimants over a period of time, John Smith will be required to provide a quarterly report to all creditors and parties in interest entitled to such payments regarding the progress of the Plan.

8.4 <u>Resolution of Disputes and Undetermined Claims or Interests</u>. Disputes regarding the proper classification of Claims not otherwise specifically classified shall be resolved pursuant to procedures established by the Bankruptcy Code, the Bankruptcy

251

Rules, and other applicable law, the Bankruptcy Court and this Plan, and such resolution shall not be a condition precedent to confirmation or consummation of this Plan.

8.5 <u>Default</u>. Any payment required to be made by a date certain under the Plan shall be made no later than 30 days following the date provided in the Plan.

8.6 <u>Current Book Accounts</u>. To the extent that John Smith has maintained current book accounts with any trade creditor post-petition, such accounts shall be reaffirmed hereunder and shall be paid according to the terms and conditions thereof in the ordinary course of business unless altered by a Court of competent jurisdiction.

 respect to such matter.

ARTICLE IX

<u>PROVISIONS FOR RETENTION OF JURISDICTION BY THE</u>

<u>BANKRUPTCY COURT FOR SUPERVISION OF THE PLAN</u>

9.1 <u>Scope of Jurisdiction</u>. The Bankruptcy Court shall retain jurisdiction over the Chapter 11 case for the following purposes:

(a) determining any and all objections to the allowance of classifications or subordinations of Claims or Interests, including all counterclaims, cross-claims or third party complaints arising therefrom (whether expressed by way of a contested matter or adversary proceeding);

(b) determining any and all fee applications and any other fees and expenses authorized to be paid or reimbursed under the Bankruptcy Code;

(c) determining any and all pending applications for the rejection or assumption of executory contracts or for any leases to which the Debtor-in-Possession is a party or with respect to which it may be liable, to set bar dates arising from the rejection of any of the same, and to hear and determine,; and if need be, to liquidate any and all claims arising therefrom;

(d) determining any and all applications, adversary proceedings, and contested or litigated matters before the Bankruptcy Court and commenced before the expiration of six months after the Consummation Date;

(e) modifying the Plan or remedying any defect or omission or reconciling any inconsistency in any order of the Bankruptcy Court including the Confirmation Order to the extent authorized by the Bankruptcy Code;

(f) determining all controversies, suits and disputes that may arise in connection with the interpretation, enforcement or consummation of this Plan;

(g) implementing the Plan, including without limitation,

entering appropriate orders to protect the Debtor-in-Possession from creditor actions;

(h) entering a final decree closing the Chapter 11 case; and

(j) determining such other matters as may arise in connection with this Plan or the Confirmation Order.

9.2 <u>Failure of the Bankruptcy Court to Exercise Jurisdiction</u>. If the Bankruptcy Court abstains from exercising, or declines to exercise jurisdiction or is otherwise without jurisdiction over any matter arising out of the Chapter 11 case, including the matters set forth in this Article, this Article shall have no effect upon and shall not control, prohibit or limit the exercise of jurisdiction by any other Court having competent jurisdiction with respect to such matter.

ARTICLE X

IMPAIRED AND UNIMPAIRED CLASSES

AND VOTING ON THE PLAN

To be confirmed, the Plan must be approved by more than fifty percent (50%) in number and sixty-six and two-thirds percent (66.67%) in dollar amount of votes actually cast by each impaired class in Classes I-II. Two-thirds in percentage of interest must approve the Plan for Class III to accept the Plan. "Impaired Class" is generally defined by the Bankruptcy Code as those classes of claimants whose legal, equitable or contractual rights are altered under the terms of the Plan.

In determining whether the Plan has been accepted by each class, votes will only be counted if submitted by a creditor whose claim is duly scheduled by the Debtor-in-Possession as undisputed, noncontingent and unliquidated, or , who has filed with the Court a proof of Claim on or before the Claims Bar Date set in this case, which has not been disallowed or suspended prior to the computation of the votes on the Plan. The Ballot form which you will receive does not constitute a proof of claim. If you are uncertain whether or not your claim has been correctly scheduled, you should check the Debtor-in-Possession's schedules which are on file in the Bankruptcy Court. The Bankruptcy Court will not provide this information over the telephone.

10.1 <u>Unimpaired Classes</u>. Class I is unimpaired under the Plan as defined by §1124 of the Bankruptcy Code. By virtue of its status as an "unimpaired" class of claims under the Bankruptcy Code, this class is deemed to have accepted the Plan in accordance with Bankruptcy Code §1126(f). Accordingly, the Debtor-in-Possession-in-Possession is not required to solicit votes of such Class with respect to the acceptance or rejection of the Plan.

10.2 <u>Impaired Voting Classes</u>. The Claims of claimants or interest holders in classes II-III are impaired by this Plan. Such claimants or interest holders shall be entitled to vote to accept or reject the Plan. A Class of claims shall have accepted the Plan if the Plan is accepted by the holders of at least two-thirds in dollar amount and more than one-half in number of the claims of each such class that vote and whose vote is received by the date fixed by the Court.

10.3 <u>Reservation of §1129(b) Rights</u>. Upon any rejections of the Plan by Classes II or III, John Smith shall request that the Bankruptcy Court confirm the Plan in accordance with §1129(b) of the Bankruptcy Code.

Under 11 U.S.C. §1129(b)(1), a plan proponent may effectuate a cramdown, confirmation of the plan over rejection by a dissenting class of claims or interests, if the Court finds that the Plan is fair and equitable and does not unfairly discriminate as to a class of claims or interests.

A plan is fair and equitable as to a class of secured claims pursuant to 11 U.S.C. §1129(b)(2)(A) if a class of secured claims retains its liens and is either paid in full over the life of the plan, paid in full from the proceeds of a sale of any property subject to the secured claim, or if the holder of a secured claim receives the indubitable value of its claim. In the present Plan, it is John Smith's contention that this test is met with respect to the secured claims in Class I.

A plan is fair and equitable with respect to a class of unsecured claims pursuant to 11 U.S.C. §1129(b)(2)(B) if the class of claims is paid in full over the life of the plan or if no junior class of claims or interests receives a dividend under the Plan. In the present Plan, it will be John Smith's contention that since all classes of claims are being paid in full that the Plan is fair and equitable with respect to all senior classes.

A plan is fair and equitable with respect to a class of interests pursuant to 11 U.S.C. §1129(b)(2)(C) if all interest holders within the class retain their interests and if no junior class receives a dividend. In the present Plan, it will be John Smith's contention, in addition to those set forth above, that the interest holders will retain no interests in John Smith inconsistent with the provisions of the Plan and consistent with the rights of all senior classes provided for under the Plan.

ARTICLE XI

CONDITIONS PRECEDENT TO CONSUMMATION

10.1 The following shall be the condition precedent to consummation of the Plan:

(a) The Confirmation Order shall have become a Final Order of the Bankruptcy Court.

257

ARTICLE XII

DISCHARGE, SURRENDER AND CANCELLATION

OF CLAIMS AND INTERESTS

12.1 Discharge of Claims. Except as otherwise provided herein or in the Confirmation Order, the rights afforded in this Plan and the payments and distributions to be made hereunder shall be in complete exchange for, and in full satisfaction, discharge and release of all existing debts and claims of any kind, nature or description whatsoever against the Debtor-in-Possession-in-Possession, or of its assets or properties; and upon the Effective Date, all existing claims against the Debtor-in-Possession-in-Possession shall be, and be deemed to be exchanged, satisfied, discharged and released in full and all holders of claims shall be precluded from asserting against the Debtor-in-Possession-in-Possession or its assets or properties any other or further claim based upon any act or omission, transaction or other activity of any kind or nature that occurred prior to the Effective Date, whether or not such holder filed a proof of claim.

12.2 Effect of Confirmation Order. Except as provided for in this Plan, the Confirmation order shall be a judicial determination of discharge of John Smith from all debts that arose before the Effective Date and any liability on a claim that is determined under Bankruptcy Code §502 as if such claim had arisen before the

Effective Date, whether or not a proof of claim based on any such debt or liability is filed under Bankruptcy Code §501 and whether or not a claim based on such debt or liability is allowed under Bankruptcy Code §502, and operates as an injunction against the commencement or continuation of an action, the employment of process of an act, to collect, recover or offset any such debt as the liability of the Debtor-in-Possession-in-Possession, whether or not discharge of such debt is waived.

12.3 <u>Surrender of Instruments and Release of Liens</u>. Except as otherwise provided in the Plan, each holder of an instrument evidencing a Claim shall surrender such instrument to the Debtor-in-Possession-in-Possession and the Debtor-in-Possession-in-Possession shall distribute to the holder thereof the distributions provided for in the Plan. No distribution under the Plan shall be made to or on behalf of any such holder of such a claim unless and until such instrument is received or the non-availability of such instrument is established to the reasonable satisfaction of the Debtor-in-Possession-in-Possession. Each Claimant who is to receive a distribution under the Plan in complete satisfaction of a Secured Claim shall not receive such distributions until such claimant executes a release of such lien in recordable form and delivers the same to the Debtor-in-Possession-in-Possession. Any such holder who fails to surrender such instrument or satisfactorily explain its non-availability or to execute such release of liens within one year of the Effective Date shall be deemed to have no further Claim and shall not participate in any distribution under this Plan.

12.4 <u>Post-Confirmation Effect of Evidence of Claim</u>. Notes and other evidences of Claims shall, upon the Effective Date, represent only the right to participate in the distributions contemplated by this Plan or matters reserved by the Plan.

ARTICLE XIII

MISCELLANEOUS

13.1 <u>Amendment</u>. The Plan may be altered, amended or modified by the Debtor-in-Possession-in-Possession before or after the Confirmation Date in the manner provided for by 11 U.S.C. §1127. A holder of a Claim or Interest that has accepted or rejected the Plan shall be deemed to have accepted or rejected, as the case may be, the Plan as modified, unless, within the time fixed by the Bankruptcy Court, such holder changes its previous acceptance or rejection.

13.2 <u>Headings</u>. The headings used in the Plan are inserted for convenience only and neither constitute a portion of the Plan nor, in any manner, affect the provisions or interpretations of the Plan.

13.3 <u>Severability</u>. Should any provision in the Plan be determined to be unenforceable, such determination shall in no way limit or affect the enforceability and operative effect of any other provision(s) of the Plan.

13.4 <u>Successors and Assigns</u>. The rights and obligations of any person named or referred to in the Plan shall be binding upon, and shall inure to the benefit of, the successors and assigns of such person.

13.5 <u>Internal References</u>. The words "herein", "hereof", "hereto", "hereunder" and other words of similar import refer to the Plan as a whole and not to any particular section, subsection or clause contained in the Plan.

13.6 <u>Notices</u>. All notices any payments required or permitted to be made in accordance with the Plan shall be in writing and shall be made by placing the notice or payment in the United States Mail with first-class postage affixed and addressed to the holder of an allowed claim at their last known address. It shall be the duty of such claimants to inform the Debtor-in-Possession of any changes in address. Failure to do so prior to completion of the Plan shall be deemed a waiver of any amounts left due and owing to such creditors.

THE FOREGOING IS A BRIEF SUMMARY OF THE PLAN AND SHOULD NOT BE RELIEF UPON FOR VOTING PURPOSES. CREDITORS ARE URGED TO READ THE

PLAN IN FULL. CREDITORS ARE FURTHER URGED TO CONSULT WITH COUNSEL, OR WITH EACH OTHER, IN ORDER TO FULLY UNDERSTAND THE PLAN. THE PLAN IS COMPLEX INASMUCH AS IT REPRESENTS A PROPOSED BINDING AGREEMENT BY DEBTOR, AND AN INTELLIGENT JUDGMENT CONCERNING SUCH PLAN CANNOT BE MADE WITHOUT UNDERSTANDING IT.

DOE & ROE

DATED:_____ By:_____

Attorneys for Debtor-in-Possession

PROJECTED STATEMENT OF PROFIT AND LOSS
FOR TWELVE MONTHS THRU DECEMBER, 1997

REVENUE	JAN	FEB	MARCH	APRIL	MAY	JUNE	JULY
SALES CONTRACT	$178,000	$189,500	$199,200	$215,792	$242,800	$310,900	$326,500
TOTAL REVENUE	$178,000	$189,500	$199,200	$215,792	$242,800	$310,900	$326,500
COST OF SALES	156,462	166,570	175,097	189,681	213,421	273,281	286,994
GROSS PROFITS	21,538	22,930	24,103	26,111	29,379	37,619	39,506
EXPENSES:							
OFFICER SALARIES	5,160	5,160	5,160	5,160	5,160	5,160	5,160
OFFICE SALARIES	4,240	4,240	4,240	4,240	4,240	4,240	4,240
ACCOUNTING & LEGAL	498	531	558	604	680	871	944
ADVERTISING	107	114	120	124	146	187	196
DEPRECIATION	516	550	578	626	704	902	947
EMPLOYEE BENEFITS	501	501	501	501	531	501	510
EQUIPMENT RENTAL	249	265	279	302	340	435	457
GAS & OIL	623	663	697	755	850	1,086	1,143
INSURANCE	2,283	2,283	2,283	2,283	2,283	2,283	2,283
INTEREST	1,066	1,066	1,066	1,066	1,066	1,066	1,066
OFFICE EXPENSE	160	171	179	194	219	280	794
RENT EXPENSE	1,052	1,052	1,052	1,052	1,052	1,052	1,052
PROMOTIONS	125	133	139	151	170	218	229
TRAVEL & ENTERTAINMENT	214	227	239	259	291	373	392
REPAIR & MAINTENANCE	498	531	552	604	669	871	914
SMALL TOOLS	427	455	478	518	563	746	784
SUPPLIES	196	208	219	237	267	342	359
POSTAGE	53	57	60	65	73	93	98
TAXES ON PAYROLL	978	978	978	978	978	978	978
TELEPHONE	392	417	438	475	534	684	178
TRASH & CLEANING	135	135	135	135	135	135	135
TRUCK EXPENSE	730	777	817	885	995	1,275	1,339
UTILITIES	53	57	60	65	73	93	98
TOTAL EXPENSES	20,256	20,571	20,828	21,279	22,019	23,871	24,296
PRETAX INCOME OR (LOSS)	1,282	2,359	3,275	4,832	7,360	13,748	15,210
CASH FLOW							
NET INCOME OR (LOSS)	1,282	2,359	3,275	4,832	7,360	13,748	15,210
SETTLEMENT PAYMENTS	4,600	4,600	4,600	4,600	4,600	4,600	4,600
BALANCE RETAINED BY BUSINESS	(3,318)	(2,241)	(1,325)	232	2,760	9,148	10,610

PROJECTED STATEMENT OF PROFIT AND LOSS
FOR TWELVE MONTHS THRU DECEMBER, 1997

REVENUE	AUG	SEPT	OCT	NOV	DEC	12 MONTH TOTAL
SALES CONTRACT	$272,900	$239,700	$190,800	$182,200	$174,700	2,722,792
TOTAL REVENUE	$272,700	$239,700	$190,800	$182,200	$174,700	2,722,792
COST OF SALES	239,679	210,696	167,713	160,154	153,561	2,393,309
GROSS PROFITS	33,021	29,004	23,087	22,046	21,139	329,483

EXPENSES:

	AUG	SEPT	OCT	NOV	DEC	12 MONTH TOTAL
OFFICER SALARIES	5,160	5,160	5,160	5,160	5,160	61,920
OFFICE SALARIES	4,240	4,240	4,240	4,240	4,240	50,880
ACCOUNTING & LEGAL	764	671	534	510	489	7,654
ADVERTISING	164	144	114	109	105	1,630
DEPRECIATION	791	695	553	528	507	7,897
EMPLOYEE BENEFITS	501	501	501	501	501	6,021
EQUIPMENT RENTAL	382	336	287	255	245	3,832
GAS & OIL	955	839	668	638	611	9,528
INSURANCE	2,283	2,283	2,283	2,283	2,283	27,396
INTEREST	1,066	1,066	1,066	1,066	1,066	12,822
OFFICE EXPENSE	246	216	172	164	157	2,952
RENT EXPENSE	1,052	1,052	1,052	1,052	1,052	12,624
PROMOTIONS	191	168	134	128	122	1,908
TRAVEL & ENTERTAINMENT	327	292	229	219	210	3,272
REPAIR & MAINTENANCE	764	671	534	510	489	7,607
SMALL TOOLS	655	575	458	437	419	6,515
SUPPLIES	300	264	210	200	192	2,994
POSTAGE	82	72	57	55	52	817
TAXES ON PAYROLL	978	978	978	978	978	11,736
TELEPHONE	616	527	420	401	384	5,466
TRASH & CLEANING	135	135	135	135	135	1,620
TRUCK EXPENSE	1,119	983	782	747	716	11,165
UTILITIES	82	72	57	55	52	817
TOTAL EXPENSES	22,853	21,940	20,624	20,371	20,165	259,073
PRETAX INCOME OR (LOSS)	10,168	7,064	2,463	1,675	974	70,410

CASH FLOW

	AUG	SEPT	OCT	NOV	DEC	12 MONTH TOTAL
NET INCOME OR (LOSS)	10,168	7,064	2,463	1,675	974	70,410
SETTLEMENT PAYMENTS	4,600	4,600	4,600	4,600	4,600	55,200
BALANCE RETAINED BY BUSINESS	5,568	2,464	(2,137)	(2,925)	(3,653)	15,183

FORM 26.4

Chapter 11 Ballot

Attorneys for Debtor-In-Possession

UNITED STATES BANKRUPTCY COURT

SOUTHERN DISTRICT OF CALIFORNIA

In re:)   CASE NO. 88-8888-Z11
)
JOHN SMITH CONTRACTING, INC.,   )   BALLOT
)
      Debtor-In-Possession   )
)
_____)

Please complete in full to receive proper voting credit. IN ORDER
TO BE COUNTED IN THE TABULATION OF BALLOTS, ALL VOTES MUST BE
RECEIVED BY THIS OFFICE BY MAY 10, 1989.
(Please type or print)

1.   NAME:_____

      ADDRESS:_____
                                   STREET

      _____
           CITY   STATE   ZIP

2.   Amount of Claim: $_____

      Class of Claim: _____

I cast my vote to :

      [   ] ACCEPT PLAN   [   ] REJECT PLAN

DATED:_____   _____
                                        SIGNATURE

WHEN COMPLETED RETURN TO:
DOE & ROE
50 MAPLE STREET
SUITE 800
SAN DIEGO, CA 92101